OECD

REVIEWS OF NATIONAL POLICIES FOR EDUCATION

IRELAND

ORGANISATION FOR ECONOMIC CO-OPERATION AND DEVELOPMENT

Pursuant to Article 1 of the Convention signed in Paris on 14th December 1960, and which came into force on 30th September 1961, the Organisation for Economic Co-operation and Development (OECD) shall promote policies designed:

— to achieve the highest sustainable economic growth and employment and a rising standard of living in Member countries, while maintaining financial stability, and thus to contribute to the development of the world economy;
— to contribute to sound economic expansion in Member as well as non-member countries in the process of economic development; and
— to contribute to the expansion of world trade on a multilateral, non-discriminatory basis in accordance with international obligations.

The original Member countries of the OECD are Austria, Belgium, Canada, Denmark, France, Germany, Greece, Iceland, Ireland, Italy, Luxembourg, the Netherlands, Norway, Portugal, Spain, Sweden, Switzerland, Turkey, the United Kingdom and the United States. The following countries became Members subsequently through accession at the dates indicated hereafter: Japan (28th April 1964), Finland (28th January 1969), Australia (7th June 1971) and New Zealand (29th May 1973). The Commission of the European Communities takes part in the work of the OECD (Article 13 of the OECD Convention). Yugoslavia takes part in some of the work of the OECD (agreement of 28th October 1961).

Publié en français sous le titre :
**EXAMENS DES
POLITIQUES NATIONALES D'ÉDUCATION :
IRLANDE**

© OECD 1991
Applications for permission to reproduce or translate all or part of this publication should be made to:
Head of Publications Service, OECD
2, rue André-Pascal, 75775 PARIS CEDEX 16, France

This report on Ireland is one of the long-established series of *Reviews of National Policies for Education.*

It is divided into three parts. Part One, the Examiners' Report, describes and discusses the Irish education system, raises issues and identifies policy options. Part Two provides a summary record of the review meeting that took place during the proceedings of the Education Committee when the Irish Delegation, led by the Ministrer of Education, Mrs Mary O'Rourke, replied to detailed questions from the examiners and Committee members. Part Three summarises the authoritative Background Report prepared by the national authorities in advance of the examiners' visit to Ireland.

The rapporteur was Mr John Lowe and the examiners were Mr Malcolm Skilbeck, Australia and Mr Michael Smith, United States.

This volume is published on the responsibility of the OECD Secretary-General.

ALSO AVAILABLE

Education in OECD Countries
A Compendium of Statistical Information 1987-1988 (1991)
(91 90 06 1) ISBN 92-64-13425-5   FF140   £17.00   US$30.00   DM55

Reviews of National Policies for Education
Higher Education in California (1990)
(91 90 02 1) ISBN 92-64-13412-3   FF140   £17.00   US$30.00   DM55
Norway (1990)
(91 90 01 1) ISBN 92-64-13315-1   FF90   £11.00   US$19.00   DM35
Spain (1987)
(91 87 01 1) ISBN 92-64-12902-2   FF90   £9.00   US$18.00   DM40
Turkey (1989)
(91 89 01 1) ISBN 92-64-13207-4   FF95   £11.50   US$20.00   DM39

Cut along dotted line

ORDER FORM

Please enter my order for:

Qty.	Title	Price
......	....	....
......	....	....
......	....	....
......	....	....
	Total :	....

- Payment is enclosed ☐
- Charge my VISA card ☐   Number of card ....
  (Note: You will be charged the French franc price.)
  Expiration of card ....   Signature ....
- *Send invoice. A purchase order is attached* ☐

Send publications to *(please print)*:
Name ....
Address ....
....
....

Send this Order Form to OECD Publications Service, 2, rue André-Pascal, 75775 PARIS CEDEX 16, France, or to OECD Publications and Information Centre or Distributor in your country *(see last page of the book for addresses)*.

Prices charged at the OECD Bookshop.
THE OECD CATALOGUE OF PUBLICATIONS *and supplements will be sent free of charge on request addressed either to OECD Publications Service, or to the OECD Distributor in your country.*

TABLE OF CONTENTS

Introduction 7
The OECD Examiners and the Irish Delegation 10

Part One

THE EXAMINERS' REPORT

1. Ireland Today 11
2. The Education System 25
3. Issues and Problems 35
4. The Schools: Organisation and Practice 53
5. The Schools, Values and the Curriculum 65
6. What Teachers? In What Numbers? In Which Institutions? .. 77
7. The Teaching Career: Training and Incentives 91

Part Two

RECORD OF THE REVIEW MEETING
Paris, 30 November 1989

1. Setting the Scene 113
2. Policies, Priorities, Resources, Planning and Control .. 117
3. The Schools: Organisation, Practice, Curriculum and Values .. 122
4. Teacher Surplus and the Training Institutions 125
5. The Teaching Career: Training and Incentives 129
6. Training for Leadership and Management 132
7. Concluding Remarks 133

Part Three

SUMMARY OF THE BACKGROUND REPORT
prepared by the Irish authorities

1.	Background and Context	137
2.	The System of Education in Ireland	138
3.	The Nature of School Provision	143
4.	The Cost of Education	145
5.	The Education and Training of Teachers	146
6.	The Employment of Teachers	148
7.	The Supply of and Demand for Teachers	150
8.	Education and the Economy	151
9.	A View of the Irish Education System: Current Issues and Problems	153

LIST OF TABLES

1.	Evolution of births in selected years: 1960-1986	14
2.	Basic statistics: international comparisons; indicators of living standards, 1985	16
3.	Firms reporting shortages of labour and of skilled labour generally in business surveys, 1973-1988	19
4.	Unemployment in the OECD area, 1987-1990	21
5.	Public expenditure on labour market programmes as a percentage of GDP, 1985-1988	46
6.	Total expenditure on education (by sources), 1985	48
7.	Public expenditure on education (including subsidies), 1985	49
8.	Current expenditure on public education (by purpose), 1985	50

LIST OF DIAGRAMS

1.	The population aged 3-24 and the population in education as percentages of the total population in 1986/87	15
2.	Enrolment rates: age group 3-6 (pre-primary and first-level education), 1985/86	26
3.	Comparison between the proportion of an age group obtaining a second level-second stage qualification allowing access to third level education and the proportion actually enrolling, 1985/86	32
4.	Percentage of GDP devoted to public expenditure on education, 1985/86	47

INTRODUCTION

It is a challenge for a team of three examiners, on the basis of necessarily limited first-hand experience, to undertake a review of education in Ireland with special reference to teacher supply and training: challenging, not only because the amount of documentary evidence available is voluminous but also because so many groups and individuals have strong views about the present condition of education and what is required to improve it. If some of these views reflect, quite understandably, partisan positions, they are founded in the main on an intimate knowledge and experience of the education system and sound analytical procedures. Thus, apart from the authoritative Background Report prepared by the Department of Education, apart from numerous oral statements heard during their short visit to Ireland, apart from documentary material provided as they moved from place to place, the examiners had at their disposal written submissions from a wide variety of organisations and several individuals covering no fewer than 936 pages. What is left for outsiders to say that has not been said already? Ireland may be geographically a small country with a small population, but it ferments with comment and controversy.

The examiners had reason to approach their task with due modesty for the further reason that they were treading in famous footsteps. Ireland was the object of the very first OECD review of national policies for education as long ago as the early 1960s, and that review remains a landmark both in the national and international memory. Its distinctive feature was the Background Report prepared by the Irish authorities under the title *Investment in Education*. That report was remarkable for its comprehensiveness, its studied detachment, its theoretical underpinning, its systematic accumulation of a mass of baseline data, its detailed estimates of quantitative trends, and not least for the originality of the methods that it used to penetrate unexplored territory. The report went out of its way to deny any prescriptive intent or explicit policy orientation and, indeed, made only one concrete proposal, namely, to establish a planning unit in the Department of Education. In reality, however, leaving the evidence to speak for itself, it indicated numerous reforms required in the national system of education. Today, no one questions in Ireland that the changes in the education system that have taken place since 1965 or so owe a huge debt to its coded recommendations.

Neither the Irish authorities nor the examiners could hope to emulate the achievement of the team that produced the highly technical report on *Investment in Education*, if only because they disposed of far less time and far fewer resources. The examiners have endeavoured, on the basis of what they have read, what they saw, and what they were told: *i)* to identify and discuss in general rather than technical terms the present and emerging issues and problems that appear to be facing Irish education and that have a bearing on the condition of teaching and teachers, to which they were invited to pay special attention; *ii)* to analyse in greater detail the specific problems of teacher supply and training.

Part One

THE EXAMINERS' REPORT

THE OECD EXAMINERS

Mr M. SKILBECK — Vice-Chancellor, Deakin University, Australia

Mr M. SMITH — Dean, School of Education, Stanford University, United States of America

Mr J. LOWE — Rapporteur, formerly of the OECD Secretariat

THE IRISH DELEGATION

Mrs Mary O'ROURKE, T.D. — Minister for Education

H. E. Mr Tadgh O'SULLIVAN — Ambassador, Permanent Representative

Mr Noel LINDSAY — Secretary of the Department of Education

Ms Margaret WALSH — Advisor to the Minister

Mr Padraig O NUALLAIN — Chief Inspector

Mr Thomas GILLEN — Assistant Secretary

Mr Sean O'BRIAIN — Assistant Secretary

Mr Torlach O'CONNOR — Chairman, Department of Education Review Team

Mr David GORDON — Private Secretary to the Minister

Mr John LAWTON — Deputy Permanent Representative

Mr John MORAHAN — Deputy Permanent Representative

Chapter 1

IRELAND TODAY

A new State and an old culture

Despite its position as a peripheral island, Ireland has long had close ties with Europe and the rest of the world. Its contribution to culture and education during its own golden period and the dark ages forms a significant element in the story of European civilisation. The monastic system that structured the schools of the middle ages carried an indelible Irish imprint, and the internationalism of that distant age is cherished in Ireland today. In the nineteenth and twentieth centuries its widespread missionary activity throughout the English-speaking world and in Africa allowed it to have widespread influence in religious and educational contexts. Large-scale emigration to many regions of the world have established an Irish cultural presence far beyond what might be expected from its geographical location and small population. It has been an active member of intergovernmental organisations. Since acceding to the Economic European Community (EEC) in 1973 Ireland has adopted a strong pro-European stance influenced by its desire for still closer links with mainland Europe and for regional support to improve its standard of living in line with other countries in the Community.

To understand contemporary Ireland, it is necessary to recognise how much its remote as well as more recent history still affects public values and attitudes and offers a key to understanding its institutions, not least its system of education. Historians and archaeologists indicate that it has been inhabited for at least 8 000 years and that it has inherited a rich legacy from its prehistoric past. The coming of Christianity among the Celtic people in the fifth century led to a remarkable flowering of religious fervour, scholarship, art and missionary endeavour. Ireland was invaded repeatedly by the Vikings from the late eighth century. The battle of Clontarf of 1014, which saw the Vikings defeated by the Irish High King, was an important turning point. The Normans invaded in the twelfth century and this evolved into conquest by the English, who became well established in the sixteenth and seventeenth centuries. English rule continued until after the First World War. The rise of Irish nationalism and conflict with England led to a partition settlement in 1922. This established Northern Ireland, comprising the six north-eastern counties that remained within the United Kingdom. The other twenty-six counties formed the new polity, the Irish Free State, changed to the Republic of Ireland in 1949. The Anglo-Irish Treaty of 1922, which established the partition settlement was not accepted by all, and a bitter civil war ensued until those supporting the Treaty enforced their authority. Conflict and difficulties continue to exist between nationalist and unionist opinion within Northern Ireland. The Government of the Republic has a consultative role with Great Britain on some of Northern Ireland's affairs through the Anglo-Irish Agreement.

Not surprisingly, given their troubled past, the Irish have an uncommonly acute sense of history and a passionate attachment to their relatively recent status as a sovereign state. They are at once proud of their cultural heritage and quick to renounce any reminder of previous colonial servitude. Their institutions are an elusive blend of pre-independence laws, regulations and institutions and post-independence innovations. As will be shown, the structure, organisation and very terminology of their education system can only be apprehended in the light of the long drawn out tensions and compromises that characterised relations between a ruling Protestant minority and a large Catholic majority.

Ireland's pride of heritage is illustrated by the endurance of Celtic culture in literature and the arts up to the present day and by a tenacious attachment to the native language. Irish or Gaelic, a Celtic language akin to Scots Gaelic and Welsh and distantly connected with Breton, fell largely into disuse during the latter part of the protracted English occupation, only to be vigorously resuscitated by a cultural revival movement in the late nineteen century. Today, the majority of the population can speak at least some Gaelic, and approximately 65 000 people, mainly living along the Atlantic coastline, use it as their vernacular language. It is the first official language; all public documents must appear in Irish and English. The custom is to begin public meetings with a salutation in Gaelic. Since 1922 one of the primary aims of education has been to encourage the spread of bilingualism.

The pride of the Irish is further illustrated by the close bonds that continue to attach to their native land the millions who have emigrated. Movement to and from the United Kingdom has always been intensive[1]. Emigration to Australia has been on a large scale. In a short space of time after the notorious potato famine of the 1840s, no fewer than 1 million people, out of the then population of 8.5 million in the whole of Ireland, emigrated to North America. Hundreds of thousands followed later in the nineteenth century. It is today a commonplace statistic that those of Irish descent living in the eastern states of America alone far outnumber the total population of Ireland. It remains the dream of the overseas Irish to visit the "old country", and overseas remittances and donations continue to make a not insignificant contribution to the national revenue.

Geographic and demographic characteristics

Ireland occupies the greater part of a temperate island. Its total area is 69 000 Km². It is separated from Great Britain by the narrow Irish Sea. It looks out to the West on the Atlantic Ocean that extends to North America 3 000 miles away. Although covering such a limited area, its road and rail communications have been, and remain, slow. Its location on the fringe of Europe, together with restricted internal mobility until recent times, help to account for the enduring strength of its indigenous culture.

The population of Ireland was 3 538 000 in April 1988, the fourth smallest among OECD countries. It is characterised by its youthfulness. Over half the population is under 25, and 30.5 per cent (1988) is under 15. Apart from Australia and Turkey, Ireland is the only OECD country to have experienced a rising birthrate until very recently. The number of births increased from 61 000 in 1960 to over 74 000 in 1980 (see Table 1). During the 1980s, though couples have been marrying at an earlier age, the birthrate has been falling. Still, the population, which had descended to a historically low point of 2.82 million in 1961, had risen to 3.5 million by 1986, partly because of the much reduced rate of emigration and the return of many families with young children. The projected population for the year 2001 is 3 472 000. Thus, as school enrolments were on the decrease almost everywhere else, enrolments in Ireland were swiftly increasing, and the pressure on resources was almost unsustainable. In 1986/87, well over a quarter of the population was undergoing full-time education or training, the highest proportion among OECD countries (see Diagram 1).

In other respects, population behaviour has paralleled trends in other countries. For one thing, there has been a rapid drift, particularly of young people, from the land to the urban centres; Dublin, the capital city, with its suburbs, accounts for almost one-third of the population. Nevertheless, internal migration has been relatively low by an overall OECD comparison, mainly because of the tradition of external migration and a high rate of home ownership, which discourages movement. The present distribution of the population is of the order of 53 per cent urban and 47 per cent rural.

A singular fact is that a country with such a limited geographical area should have the lowest population density (50 inhabitants per Km²) among the EEC group of countries. By contrast, in County Donegal, which lies along the north-west coast, where the land is infertile and manufacturing industry is limited, there is a high density of population for a predominantly rural area.

Emigration is a phenomenon that has historically coloured, and continues to colour, Irish life. During the 1950s it was on a large scale. The net rate slowed to a trickle during the period of economic prosperity between the early 1960s and the late 1970s, but has quickened again during the 1980s as young people have tried their luck abroad rather than run the risk of unemployment now or in the short-term future or of having to accept a level of employment well below their expectations. Net emigration

Table 1. **Evolution of births in selected years: 1960-1986**
In 000s

Country	1960	1965	1970	1975	1980	1986	% change 1960-1986
Australia	230	223	258	233	226	243	+ 6
Austria	126	130	112	94	91	87	– 31
Belgium	156	155	141	119	125	117	– 25
Canada	479	419	370	358	371	378	– 21
Denmark	76	86	71	72	57	55	– 28
Finland	82	78	65	66	63	61	– 26
France	816	862	850	745	800	779	– 5
Germany	969	1 044	811	601	621	626	– 35
Greece	157	151	145	142	148	113	– 28
Iceland	49	47	40	44	45	39	– 20
Ireland	**61**	**63**	**64**	**68**	**74**	**61**	**0**
Italy	923	1 108	917	842	658	562	– 39
Japan	1 606	1 839	1 948	1 897	1 589	1 383	– 14
Luxembourg	50	53	44	40	42	43	– 14
Netherlands	239	245	239	178	181	185	– 23
New Zealand	63	60	62	57	51	53	– 16
Norway	62	66	65	56	51	52	– 16
Portugal	214	210	181	180	161	127	– 41
Spain	655	668	656	669	566	451[a]	– 31
Sweden	102	123	110	104	97	102	0
Switzerland	94	112	99	79	74	76	– 19
United Kingdom	918	997	904	698	754	755	– 18
United States	4 307	3 801	3 739	3 144	3 589	3 731	– 13

a) 1985.
Source: OECD demographic data base.

averaged 18 700 between 1981 and 1988 and was estimated at 32 000 for 1987. Many young people intend to emigrate for good: others seek jobs abroad as a mind-broadening and end-of-education experience but, having found rewarding employment, decide not to return. Disturbing for the authorities is the tendency of many highly qualified young people to disappear from the home labour market, a case of a relatively poor country transferring valuable human capital to wealthier countries. The outflow of young people is recognised to be potentially critical in the longer term for a balanced distribution of the age groups in the population. It is also a matter of human concern to parents and families that so many young people feel compelled to leave their homeland.

The economy

For much of this century the Irish economy was stagnant and insulated within a protected market. From the late 1950s, however, until the first swingeing oil-price

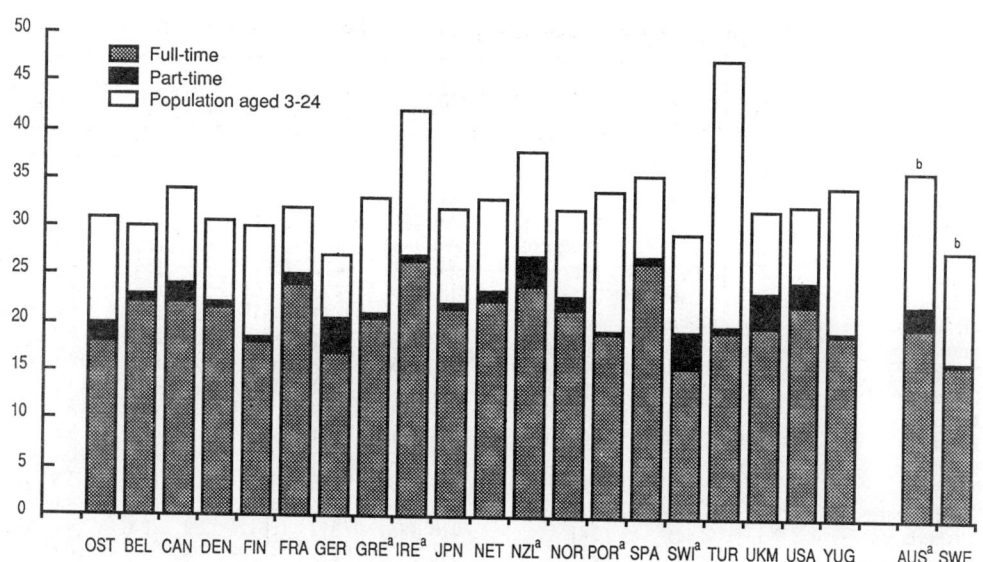

Diagram 1. **THE POPULATION AGED 3-24 AND THE POPULATION IN EDUCATION AS PERCENTAGES OF THE TOTAL POPULATION in 1986-87**

a) 1985-86.
b) Excluding pre-primary.

Source: *Education in OECD countries 1986-87 - A Compendium of Statistical Information*, OECD, Paris, 1989, p.13.

increase in 1973, Ireland enjoyed a period of sustained economic prosperity with heavy expenditure on social services and an unprecedentedly high standard of living. The annual growth rate was around 4 per cent. A policy of liberalisation, modernisation and intensive exploitation of domestic natural resources was vigorously pursued, and the economy was opened up to foreign investment.

The Industrial Development Authority has played a conspicuously dynamic role in generating foreign as well as domestic investment. Indeed, much of the economic development has been generated by foreign investment, which has been on a princely scale. Hundreds of foreign firms have been located. This foreign invasion is viewed essentially as a blessing but also as potentially harmful to domestically impelled growth. One of the main reasons given for Ireland's attraction for external companies is the existence of a well-educated and co-operative workforce. Foreign investment, notably from Japan and the United States, has been sustained at a high rate throughout the recent recession.

Thanks to the economic resurgence, per capita income rose from US$ 1 360 in 1970 to 4 394 in 1979, and to 7 541 in 1987. This still leaves Ireland as one of the poorer OECD Member countries in terms of living standards (Table 2).

Table 2. **Basic statistics: international comparisons - indicators of living standards 1985**

Countries	Private consump. per capita using US$[a]	Passenger cars, per 1 000 inhabitants	Telephones, per 1 000 inhabitants	Television sets per 1 000 inhabitants	Doctors per 1 000 inhabitants	Infant mortality per 1 000 live births
Australia	7 389	..	548 (83)	..	..	9.2 (84)
Austria	6 535	306 (81)	460 (83)	300 (81)	1.7 (82)	11.0
Belgium	7 593	335 (84)	414 (83)	303 (84)	2.8 (84)	9.4
Canada	10 059	421 (82)	664 (83)	471 (80)	1.8 (82)	9.1 (83)
Denmark	7 236	293	783	392	2.5 (84)	7.9
Finland	6 966	329 (86)	615	370 (86)	2.3 (86)	5.8 (86)
France	7 796	369 (86)	614 (86)	394 (86)	2.3 (86)	7.0 (86)
Germany	7 374	441 (86)	641 (86)	377 (86)	2.5 (84)	9.1
Greece	4 273	127	373	158 (80)	2.8 (83)	14.1
Iceland	9 930	431	525 (83)	303	2.4 (84)	5.7
Ireland	**4 378**	**206 (83)**	**235 (83)**	**181 (80)**	**1.3 (82)**	**8.9**
Italy	7 543	355 (84)	448 (84)	244 (84)	3.6 (82)	10.9
Japan	7 623	221 (83)	535 (83)	250 (80)	1.3 (82)	5.9 (84)
Luxembourg	8 694	439 (87)	425 (86)	336 (83)	1.9 (86)	9.0
Netherlands	7 461	341	410 (86)	317 (86)	2.2 (84)	9.6 (86)
New Zealand	6 236	455	646	291	2.4	10.8
Norway	8 155	382 (86)	622 (84)	346 (86)	2.2	8.5 (86)
Portugal	4 167	135 (82)	166 (83)	140 (80)	1.8 (82)	17.8
Spain	5 521	252	381 (86)	256 (82)	3.4 (86)	7.0 (84)
Sweden	7 273	377	890 (83)	390	2.5	6.8
Switzerland	9 349	402	1 334	337	1.4 (84)	6.9
Turkey	2 844	18 (82)	55 (83)	76 (79)	1.5 (83)	..
United Kingdom	7 731	312 (83)	521 (84)	336 (84)	0.5 (83)	9.4

a) 1987 for all countries under this heading.
Source: OECD Economic Outlook 1989.

After 1973 the economic situation deteriorated; the public and foreign debt swelled, culminating in a balance of payments crisis by the end of the 1970s and very high inflation. Wages and productivity stagnated. Taxation became severe.

During the past three years the economy has staged a remarkable recovery thanks to a policy of drastic retrenchment and tight fiscal controls[2]. The trade deficit has been turned into a surplus. Interest rates have dropped. GDP grew by nearly 4.5 per cent in 1987; a growthrate of 4 per cent was foreseen for the year 1989. Export earnings increased by 13.25 per cent in 1987. Inflation has declined to the lowest level since the early 1960s. However, the economic future is still viewed with caution, and the government continues to impose an austerity programme that affects all areas of public expenditure, not least that of education which is having to cope with severe resource constraints.

At the same time, no one questions the critical importance of education and training for the vitality of the economy and the entire development process. Ireland sets much store by the quality of its "human resources". Public documents contain frequent references to the vital need for a well-qualified workforce in this age of high technology. A recent report on manpower policy declared:

> "The education system, in combination with the training system, provides the economy with the skills and knowledge with which to develop and remain competitive. Post-compulsory education and training is of special importance to manpower policy because it provides the base from which most young people enter the labour market or proceed to further specialised education and training"[3].

It is commonly agreed that the commitment to education as an economic investment as well as an intrinsic good was triggered off by the first OECD review of Ireland's education policies, which took place in the early 1960s[4]. For that review the Irish authorities prepared a background report, Investment in Education (1966), which is still treated as a *locus classicus*.

Some educationists express concern about what they perceive as too strong an emphasis in recent years on the links between education and the economy and on curbing educational expenditure[5]. They fear that Irish education is being skewed towards functional, instrumentalist goals at the expense of the wider perennial aims of education, and refer to the rise of a "new vocationalism". It is the examiners' view that, while their concern may serve as a valuable corrective to any undue instrumentalist tendencies, the present balance between overall educational priorities and economic or manpower imperatives is satisfactory in general terms. Ireland has had no choice but to develop its industrial capacity at speed, and this has necessitated a drive to expand vocational and technical education and enhance its quality. But it is essential to note that this expansion has been accompanied by a parallel drive to widen access to post-compulsory general education in the cause of equality of opportunity. As to the pursuit of cost-effectiveness in the financing and management of education, this reflects the contemporary drive throughout OECD countries to keep public expenditure, which had grown out of hand during the expansionist years, within tenable bounds. Whether the particular mix -- or differential -- of general and vocational education is right is therefore a matter for debate. It is certainly relevant to policies for teacher education, the main concern of this report.

Structure of the labour market and unemployment

The period of economic growth was accompanied by fundamental changes in the size and structure of the labour market. The workforce, which had been more or less stable between 1961 and 1971, increased by 9 per cent to 1 235 000 by 1979; between 1975 and 1979 it grew at an annual average of 1.6 per cent or 18 000 jobs a year. This was all the more remarkable in that the school-leaving age had been raised from 14 to 15 in 1972, and that large numbers of teenagers who would previously have sought employment were staying on at school beyond the end of compulsory schooling.

Manufacturing industry raised employment at an annual rate of 1.7 per cent between 1961 and 1979; chemicals and plastics rose at a rate of 4 per cent. In 1987 "Manufacturing accounted for the bulk of industrial growth, rising by 11.5 per cent. Within industry, the high-technology sectors remained the fastest growing sectors, notably office machinery and data-processing equipment, which raised production by 37.5 per cent"[6]. At the same time, the numbers employed in manufacturing declined by 3 000. The overall increase in industrial employment has been paralleled by declining employment in clothing and textiles, boots and shoes, and timber products.

In 1961, 42 per cent of the workforce was still employed in agriculture. By 1987 that percentage had fallen to 15.7 per cent, despite the spectacular boom in agricultural productivity following Ireland's accession to the EEC in 1973. Agriculture, notably cattle raising and dairy farming, remains important but had already yielded to manufacturing as the main source of foreign earnings by 1969. There are still about 200 000 holdings, although many are scarcely profitable and their proprietors are an ageing group. To the eye of the traveller the Irish landscape remains overwhelmingly rural in character.

As in other countries there has been a sharp fall in the demand for manual labour, especially for that of the unskilled and semi-skilled. Qualifications have become increasingly important as employers have sought for skilled and well educated workers. At the same time, there is today only a minimal lack of skilled labour (Table 3).

In the aggregate, the number of self-employed persons has diminished. Yet nearly all new employment has been generated by small enterprises, which have proliferate throughout the country.

The major transformation has been in the service sector (53 per cent of the labour force in 1987) and in white-collar jobs. There has been a sharp rise in employment in retail and trade, financing, banking and insurance and in tourism, which has become extensive and well organised. Insurance, finance and business services expanded employment at an average rate of 4.5 per cent between 1961 and 1979. The health sector has expanded, so also has the education sector that is the object of this report.

Table 3. **Firms reporting shortages of labour and of skilled labour generally in business surveys, 1973 to 1988**

Percentage of survey firms

	Skilled labour shortage							General labour bottleneck			
	Canada	Finland	Ireland	Norway	New Zealand[a]	Sweden	United Kingdom[b]	Australia	New Zealand	Denmark	France
1973		41.5	15.8		−50.3	41.1	36.0	33.5	45.8	50.3	
1974		47.5	16.5	13.0	−21.3	58.2	35.3	24.3	38.8	15.0	
1975		44.0	8.0	4.5	19.0	41.7	16.7	6.3	11.8	4.3	
1976	12.6	16.0	9.3	3.5	−1.3	35.8	13.1	6.5	10.8	9.0	
1977	8.6	2.5	10.5	3.0	1.3	22.0	19.4	6.3	8.3	6.8	
1978	9.8	2.8	18.9	3.3	−1.8	19.3	21.7	5.5	3.3	12.8	
1979	11.8	16.3	20.6	5.0	−24.5	37.1	21.1	6.8	7.5	24.0	5.0
1980	13.0	34.3	6.9	6.8	−6.3	45.4	8.4	9.5	2.0	6.8	5.0
1981	12.7	24.0	3.6	5.8	−18.3	20.8	2.5	12.3	6.8	2.8	2.5
1982	4.7	13.3	2.3	3.3	−10.5	13.1	3.0	4.3	5.0	0.8	4.0
1983	2.0	11.5	3.0	0.3	2.8	18.3	4.4	1.0	1.8	0.8	4.0
1984	2.8	18.0	1.3	0.8	−37.0	30.0	8.2	3.5	8.8	1.8	3.0
1985	3.4	26.8	0.3	4.3	−47.5	31.3	13.2	7.8	11.5	5.8	3.8
1986	4.8	25.5	0.3	4.8	−25.3	33.8	11.7	8.3	9.3	5.0	2.5
1987	5.7	29.5	0.4	4.8	−15.3	44.8	14.2	10.8	5.8	2.3	1.8
1988	10.0	31.0	0.6	2.0	19.0	59.0	22.0	13.0	1.3	1.7	4.3

a) The skilled labour shortage series for New Zealand is a skilled labour "tendency", for which more positive numbers represent recession conditions.
b) Data are for Great Britain only.
Source: OECD Main Economic Indicators data base.

It is noteworthy that the employment of younger adults as a sectoral group differs markedly from that of older adults in terms of occupational categories. A small minority in agriculture, forestry and fishing, they have a large share of manufacturing, commerce, finance, insurance and business services. They have benefited most from grant-aided industrial development. Thus, their share of jobs created by the activities of the Industrial Development Authority has been out of all proportion to their numbers as a percentage of the labour force. According to the OECD report on youth unemployment: "...the heart of Irish employment policy has been the creation of jobs through the establishment of new enterprises and it is the young who have benefited disproportionately from the fruits of this strategy"[7]. The same report also points out:

> "When new jobs are created, young people (who are generally better educated and likely to be better trained, due to the overwhelmingly youth-oriented efforts of AnCO [Industrial Training Authority] and to the out-migration of skilled workers in earlier decades) are competing at an advantage"[8].

Being better educated and trained can be a mixed blessing for young people, however, because it means that they may have difficulty not only in finding a job but in finding one that is commensurate with their expectations. If many more talented young people are not to be driven to emigrate it is evident that challenging, or at least satisfactory, jobs must be available to them. This implies, in turn, that employers must make a conscious effort to render jobs more attractive.

Historically, unemployment and under-employment have been endemic in Ireland. However, from the late 1950s up to the mid-1970s, prolonged growth ensured a relatively high level of employment. Many more women came into the labour market and many married couples both went out to work. Thus, the participation rate of married women, which had been 5.3 per cent in 1961, had risen to over 15 per cent by 1979. In 1973, unemployment was as low as around 5.5 per cent of the workforce. Thereafter, the sluggish economic growth led to steadily rising unemployment. By 1987, approximately 232 000, or over 17 per cent, were unemployed. That percentage would have been considerably greater but for the resumption of a significant rate of emigration and the decision of many young people to spend at least some time abroad on leaving the education system. In 1988, there was an encouraging decline in the unemployment rate (see Table 4), but it remained among the highest in OECD countries.

The higher rate of unemployment has been caused by the continuing decline of jobs in agriculture, the falling demand for manual labour, the disappearance of "classical" jobs in commerce and the recent cut-back in expenditure that has led to a reduction in public sector posts and an embargo on filling vacancies.

Unemployment is most serious among the unqualified and unskilled -- as it was already in 1961 -- and among the young[9], although, as stressed in the OECD report already cited: "the ratio of youth to adult unemployment rates has been below the average of many other OECD countries"[10]. Unemployment also affects many who are qualified, not least, as will be seen, school teachers. The state regards it as the most serious of all the problems facing society; public opinion polls rate it second only to health as the major national concern.

Most other OECD countries will benefit from a decrease in youth unemployment during the next five years or so as the numbers of school-leavers fall sharply. Ireland cannot rely on the same respite in the short term, since large cohorts of young people will continue to enter the labour force each year. However, Ireland can be sure of relief before 2000. Meanwhile, it will intensify its efforts to create new jobs through industrial development. It will continue to raise the general level of education and expand its provision for training. Besides treating the employment needs of the young as a high priority, it will be seeking to do more for the long-term unemployed and to intensify training programmes for older adults, who must master new skills in order to retain their jobs or secure new ones.

Table 4. **Unemployment in the OECD area**[a]

	1987	1979-86	1987	1988	1989	1990	1979-86	1987	1988	1989	1990
	000s	Per cent of labour force[b]					Millions				
North America	**8 575.9**	**7.9**	**6.4**	**5.7**	**5½**	**5¾**	**9.7**	**8.6**	**7.7**	**7¾**	**8**
Canada	1 165.8	9.6	8.9	7.8	7¾	7¾	1.2	1.2	1.0	1	1
United States	7 410.2	7.7	6.2	5.5	5¼	5½	8.6	7.4	6.7	6¾	7
Japan	**1 734.8**	**2.4**	**2.9**	**2.5**	**2¼**	**2¼**	**1.4**	**1.7**	**1.5**	**1½**	**1½**
Central and Western Europe	**8 959.1**	**8.0**	**9.1**	**8.3**	**7¾**	**7¾**	**7.6**	**9.0**	**8.2**	**7¾**	**7¾**
Austria	130.2	2.8	3.8	3.5	3¼	3	0.1	0.1	0.1	0	0
Belgium	466.0	10.8	11.1	10.0	9½	9	0.5	0.5	0.4	½	½
France	2 516.9	8.4	10.5	10.1	10	10¼	2.0	2.5	2.4	2½	2½
Germany	2 229.0	6.3	7.9	7.9	7½	7	1.7	2.2	2.2	2	2
Ireland	231.0	12.5	17.5	16.7	15½	15	0.2	0.2	0.2	¼	¼
Luxembourg	2.7	1.2	1.6	1.4	1¼	1½	0.0	0.0	0.0	0	0
Netherlands[c]	451.0	11.4	8.7	8.3	8	8	0.6	0.5	0.4	½	½
Switzerland	23.5	0.6	0.7	0.7	¾	¾	0.0	0.0	0.0	0	0
United Kingdom	2 908.8	9.5	10.2	8.2	7	7¼	2.6	2.9	2.3	2	2
Southern Europe	**9 248.3**	**12.0**	**13.7**	**13.7**	**13½**	**13¾**	**7.7**	**9.2**	**9.3**	**9½**	**9½**
Greece	286.0	5.7	7.4	7.6	7¾	8	0.2	0.3	0.3	¼	¼
Italy	2 832.5	8.6	11.0	11.0	11	11½	2.1	2.8	2.9	3	3
Portugal	317.2	8.1	7.1	5.6	5½	5½	0.4	0.3	0.3	¼	¼
Spain	2 956.6	16.5	20.5	19.5	18¼	17¼	2.2	3.0	2.9	2¾	2½
Turkey	2 856.0	15.4	15.2	15.9	16¾	17¼	2.7	2.9	3.0	3¼	3½
Nordic countries	**482.2**	**4.4**	**4.0**	**4.1**	**4¼**	**4½**	**0.5**	**0.5**	**0.5**	**½**	**½**
Denmark	221.9	8.7	7.8	8.6	9½	9¾	0.2	0.2	0.2	¼	¼
Finland	130.3	5.2	5.1	4.5	3¾	3¾	0.1	0.1	0.1	0	0
Iceland	0.7	0.7	0.5	1.0	1¼	¾	0.0	0.0	0.0	0	0
Norway	45.4	2.4	2.1	3.2	4¼	4	0.0	0.0	0.1	0	0
Sweden	84.0	2.3	1.9	1.6	1½	1¼	0.1	0.1	0.1	0	0
Oceania	**694.7**	**6.8**	**7.4**	**7.0**	**6¾**	**7**	**0.6**	**0.7**	**0.7**	**¾**	**¾**
Australia	628.8	7.5	8.0	7.1	6½	7	0.5	0.6	0.6	½	½
New Zealand	65.8	3.7	4.1	6.0	7	7½	0.1	0.1	0.1	0	0
OECD Europe	**18 689.5**	**9.1**	**10.5**	**10.1**	**9¾**	**9¾**	**15.6**	**18.7**	**18.1**	**17¾**	**17¾**
EEC	**15 419.5**	**9.2**	**10.8**	**10.2**	**9¾**	**9½**	**12.7**	**15.4**	**14.6**	**14**	**14**
Total OECD	**29 694.9**	**7.6**	**7.8**	**7.3**	**7**	**7¼**	**27.6**	**29.7**	**28.0**	**27½**	**28¼**

a) For sources and definitions, see *OECD Economic Outlook,* No. 45, June 1989. *b)* The rates are not necessarily compatible between countries. *c)* Values for 1987 and 1988 use the new national measurement method.

Source: *OECD Employment Outlook 1989,* OECD, Paris, p. 18.

Ireland and Europe

Ireland acceded to the EEC in 1973. It is an ardent supporter of European integration and a freely acknowledged net beneficiary of the EEC's largesse. It has gained handsomely from the Common Agricultural Policy and the European Social Fund, which has helped subsidise its anti-unemployment measures and policies for regional development. A number of key initiatives in education and training have been largely financed from EEC sources. There are those who fear that Ireland has perhaps relied too much on this external support, which distorts market forces and cannot be guaranteed to continue indefinitely, and who believe that in the future it should be prepared to rely to a greater extent on domestic financing.

In general, there is now, as throughout Irish history, a widespread feeling of affinity with European culture. In education and training, however, it is argued by some critics that insufficient is being done in practical terms to reinforce the nation's adherence to the EEC. They allege that the teaching of foreign languages is inadequate, that the curriculum is not suitably internationalist in outlook, and that, in general, young people are not being fully prepared to take advantage of the economic opportunities that are confidently expected to arise after 1992. At the same time, it is to be noted that some schools have established flourishing exchange programmes and that many Irish teachers are working in EEC countries.

Social and cultural change

In spite of the rapid pace of its economic development in recent times, Ireland has preserved a distinctive national culture and traditional moral values and mores to a degree not found in many other industrialised countries. It has not been immune, however, from the pressures that have revolutionised societies in other countries: the effects of rapid urbanisation, unprecedented social mobility, foreign travel, the impact of technology, the invasion of the mass media, single-parent households (although divorce is not allowed, there has been much family break-down), increasing crime and drug abuse in the inner cities. Indeed, because its social controls had historically been so powerful, Ireland, like Japan, now regards as deeply disturbing manifestations of errant behaviour that some other countries would regard as mild. In its submission, University College, Dublin, sums up the educational consequences of social change in a suitably restrained fashion (for the purposes of this review, all references to a "submission" refer to the submissions made to the Department of Education by a wide variety of public and private bodies as well as certain individuals):

"...the very nature of what is normally acceptable behaviour, the nature of authority, discipline and, perhaps, of the pupil himself are changing too, in ways that are far from being fully understood, so that ruling assumptions so long built into educational institutions and structures may no longer apply"[11].

Ireland is overwhelmingly a Catholic country. Over 90 per cent of the population are declared Catholics. Approximately 4 per cent of the population are Protestants, and it is worth noting that around 50 per cent of them are young people in formal education. Religion continues to play a pre-eminent role in society, not least in the realm of education.

But if cultural and social changes have been less pronounced than elsewhere, a fact that partly accounts for Ireland's appeal to discriminating tourists, they have still been profound enough to shake some of the assumptions on which the organisation, delivery and content of education are based. Society has become more pluralist; there is increasing dissent; there are the beginnings of multiculturalism; there is heightened sensitivity about social-class and gender discrimination; there is a sharper focus on individual rather than group satisfaction. As will be seen, educational institutions and teachers are in the demanding situation of being expected to help conserve all that is best in the Irish way of life -- its lively arts, its powerful oral and literary tradition, its enchanting countryside and distinctive rural life -- while adapting the curriculum and their relations with pupils and students to contemporary realities.

NOTES AND REFERENCES

1. "The annual number of movements into and out of Ireland, not counting transit passengers, was of the order of seventeen million in 1964" (quoted in OECD, *Investment in Education: Ireland*, Paris, 1966, p. 25).
2. The latest OECD *Economic Survey of Ireland* (Paris, 1989, p. 9) comments favourably: "The vigorous efforts to tackle the deficit problem, in conjunction with an improving external environment, had a very rapid favourable effect on the economy. There has been a remarkable turnaround in both domestic and foreign confidence concerning the prospects of the Irish economy, compared with the pessimistic views prevailing until 1987".
3. National Economic and Social Council, *Manpower Policy in Ireland* (Dublin, 1985) p. 5.
4. "For us in Ireland this report has had an immediate impact on policy. We are now embarked on the long and arduous task of adapting our educational system and institutions to serve the needs of the nation in the age of technology and, we hope, rapid economic growth". cf. Introduction to *Investment in Education, op. cit.*, page v., by Mr. George Colley, Irish Minister of Education.
5. See, for example, the analysis of Rev. Dr. Simon Clyne, C.M., OECD Review, *Submissions*, pp. 876-877.
6. *Economic Review and Outlook 1988* (Dublin, 1988) p. 13.
7. OECD, *Improving Youth Employment Opportunities: Policies for Ireland and Portugal* (Paris, 1984) p. 43.
8. *Ibid.*, p.49.
9. "Unskilled manual employment is an extremely unreliable outlet and becoming more so. As a result those attempting to enter employment without moderate literacy, numeracy and manual skills -- those who 'drop out' of school early or fail their junior cycle exams -- are doomed to unemployment or to very unstable employment throughout their lives", (*cf.* Hannan, D., *Schooling in the Labour Market: Young People in Transition from School to Work*, Shannon Curriculum Development Centre, 1986, p. 20).
10. *Improving Youth Employment Opportunities, op.cit.*, p. 35.
11. OECD Review, *Submissions*, p. 106.

Chapter 2

THE EDUCATION SYSTEM

Recent evolution

The evolution of the education system has shadowed the evolution of the economy. It is commonly agreed that from the birth of independence up to 1960 the system was both static and gravely under-resourced. In the compulsory sector many of the classes were much too large and the curriculum was much too narrow: it is recorded that in 1957-58, 22 per cent of teachers were untrained. The upper secondary sector was small, fee-paying, and catered largely for the children of better-off parents. Higher education was elitist. The public was not inquisitive about what happened inside the system, though deeply respectful of it. The over-riding priority of the State was to promote the national language; beyond that it had no active policies. There was no "education act" nor is there one today.

The beginning of economic expansion signalled a watershed for education. The public began to display rising interest in its outcomes. The State assumed an increasingly interventionist role. The notion of investment in education for growth and development took firm root. Society embraced the ideal of equality of educational opportunity. The social demand for education increased apace. Money was found to build new schools and post-secondary institutions, and thousands of new teachers were appointed. The system expanded up to the mid-1980s when the policy of austerity called a halt; some expansion still continued in programmes oriented towards the labour market.

The education system that will now be described in summary form is much larger and more diversified than the system of thirty years ago. However, it has been supplemented rather than restructured. Most of the old strata and perennial features remain discernible.

Pre-schooling

A striking feature of Irish education is the long-standing commitment to early schooling. The "pre-school" (commonly called the infant school) is treated as a part of the national compulsory school provision and curriculum. Although primary schooling does not start until the age of six, virtually all young children attend school from the age of five (see Diagram 2) and approximately 65 per cent do so from the age of four. In effect, all children spend seven years being educated continuously up to the end of primary school, and two-thirds spend eight years. Some young people will complete no fewer than fourteen years of schooling from four to eighteen.

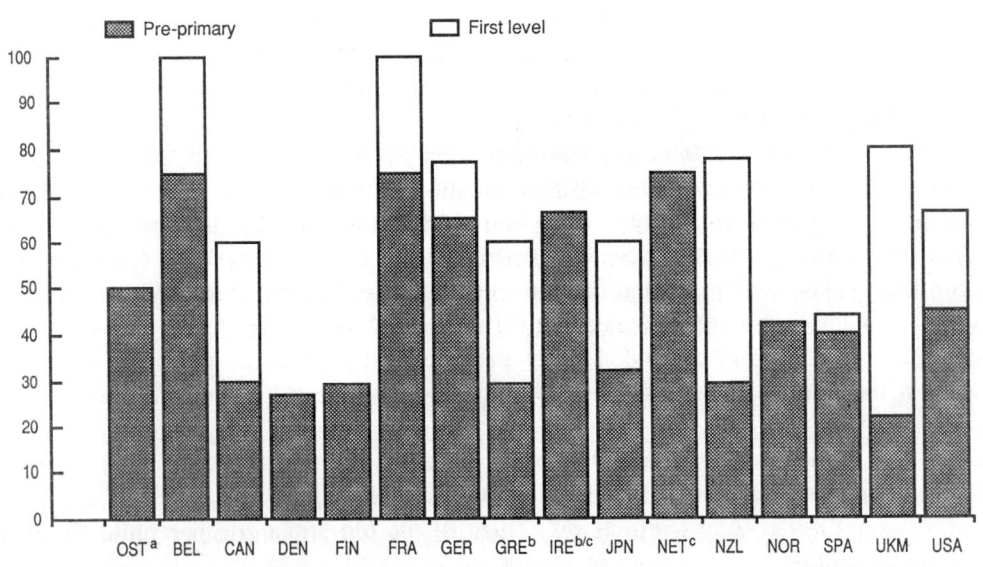

Diagram 2. **ENROLMENT RATES: AGE GROUP 3-6**
(Pre-primary and first-level education)
1985-86

a) No data for first level.
b) 1984-85.
c) Pre-primary and first level.

Source: "Education in OECD Countries 1985-86: Comparative Statistics", OECD, Paris, 1988 (General Distribution).

Compulsory schooling

Compulsory schooling extends over nine years from the age of 6 to 15, and is divided into a six-year primary and a three-year lower secondary cycle. Although there is no longer any terminal examination at the end of the primary phase, a pupil may not proceed to the secondary level without having satisfactorily completed it; few pupils are now held back. The primary cycle is commonly referred to as "first-level"[1].

A distinction must be drawn between compulsory "education" and compulsory "schooling", since parents are at liberty to have their children educated at home provided that minimum learning standards and satisfactory moral training can be assured. This reflects the priority accorded by the Irish Constitution to the right of parents to arrange for the education of their children "in their homes or in private schools or in schools recognised or established by the State". It also conforms with the fundamental tenet of the teaching of the Catholic Church, endorsed by the second Vatican Council, which recognises the "primary and inalienable right" of parents "to enjoy fullest liberty in their choice of school for their children".

Parents may send their children to any school of their choice no matter where it is located, provided that accommodation is available. In addition, groups of parents and others are free, in principle, to set up their own schools and to receive the statutory subventions of the State, subject to the general regulations applying to all schools.

Primary schools are nearly all denominational in their intake and management, and located in parishes. Notwithstanding, no child may be refused enrolment on the ground of religion in any school where a place is available. The association of primary schools with parishes is of very long standing[2].

The ultimate responsibility for each primary school lies with the "patron" who is, as a rule, the Bishop of the relevant denomination. He delegates managerial authority to a school board. Prior to 1975 there were individual school managers, usually the parish priest (Catholic) or rector or minister (Protestant). Since that date, responsibility rests with the board for the day-to-day running of each school, the right to appoint teachers, repairs and maintenance, and application of the rules laid down by the Minister of Education.

Recently, a new type of school management has emerged under the indicative rubric of *Educate Together*. The purpose is to set up new primary schools that shall be:

"Multi-denominational, in which Catholic, Protestant and other children have equal right of access, and in which each child's social, cultural and religious background is equally respected; co-educational; democratically managed"[3].

So far, there are no more than eight such schools but others are being planned. Interestingly enough, the original intention when the primary (national) schools were established in 1831 was to uphold the principle of multi-denominationalism:

"The system of National Education affords combined secular and separate religious instruction to children of all (*sic*) religions, and no attempt is made to interfere with the religious tenets of any pupils"[4].

Compulsory schooling is free of charge, but parents are required to pay for textbooks and necessary equipment. There is a free book scheme for needy pupils.

In 1987/88 there were over 3 000 primary schools, and 21 125 teachers. Approximately, 441 000 pupils were in attendance[5]. The average pupil/teacher ratio was 26.8 : 1. Enrolments are falling. 576 schools are single sex. And many schools are very small.

A substantially revised primary school curriculum was introduced in 1971. Largely designed by the primary school inspectorate, it was intended to offer an integrated range of subjects comprising: Art and Crafts, English Language, Irish Language, Mathematics, Music, Physical Education, Religious Instruction and Social and Environmental Studies. Teaching was to become child-centered and to that end there was to be flexible timetabling and methods of instruction, with emphasis on individual and small-group learning. The outcome of the curricular reform and proposals for further reform are discussed below in Chapter 5.

Religious education is distinguished from secular education and accorded the highest priority in the *Rules for National Schools*:

"Of all parts of a school curriculum Religious Instruction is by far the most important, as its subject matter, God's honour and service, includes the proper use of all man's faculties, and affords the most powerful inducements to their proper use. Religious instruction is, therefore, a fundamental part of the school course, and a religious spirit should inform and vivify the whole work of the school"[6].

Parents can exercise the right to withdraw their children from religious instruction if they so choose.

Secondary education

At the end of primary schooling there is no formal examination. Virtually all proceed directly to secondary education, commonly referred to as "second-level" or "post-primary" education. The complete secondary cycle may extend over five or six years. Almost 92 per cent of the age cohort continue in full-time education after the compulsory cycle. Some 88.7 per cent of 16 year-olds, 69.1 per cent of 17 year-olds and 42.2 per cent of 18 year-olds are now in full-time education, including apprenticeships. These percentages have been increasing progressively.

Until 1967 it was necessary to pay a tuition fee -- though sometimes minimal -- in order to attend a secondary school. After that date most secondary education tuition became free of charge and a school transport system was introduced, although parents continued to pay for other costs. Against the background of rising economic prosperity, there was an explosion in the participation rate. The attendance doubled between 1960 and 1970. Between 1963 and 1986 it almost trebled from 118 893 to 330 000. There was a marked increase in the number of girls. New types of school were created to match the rising demand. As a result, there are now five types of school at the secondary level: *secondary (sic), vocational, comprehensive, community and community college.*

Approximately two-thirds of all second level schools are *secondary schools* (sometimes referred to as voluntary secondary schools). These are mostly of small to medium size. Ten per cent have under 200 students and only fourteen schools have over 800 students. They are privately owned and managed, mostly by religious orders, but receive from the State the full costs of each recognised teacher's salary, except for an annual contribution of £400. They also receive a capitation grant for each student and 90 per cent of the cost of buildings and equipment. They belong to the tradition of classical grammar schools but have been steadily broadening and modernising their curricula in recent years. A few of them are wholly or partially residential.

Vocational schools were established originally in order to provide a strictly job-oriented curriculum of vocational and technical subjects but now offer the complete range of secondary subjects and cater for adults as well as young people. They are controlled by thirty eight regionally based and locally elected Vocational Education Committees (created in 1930), and financed up to 90 per cent by the State. Each Committee consists of fourteen members of which 5 to 8 must be nominated by the local authority.

Comprehensive schools, which date from 1966, were set up to meet the needs of neighbourhoods where no secondary level education was otherwise available. They offer a wide-ranging curriculum, including technical and vocational subjects. They are controlled by the Department of Education, and are financed 100 per cent by the State.

Community schools date only from 1973 and, like the North American model, are designed to serve as centres for all neighbourhood educational and cultural activities. These, too, come under the influence of the Department of Education and are wholly financed by the State. They offer the same broad curriculum as comprehensive schools. The designation of *community college* is now being used to describe new or expanded vocational schools.

All five types of secondary school today offer a broad curriculum but with different emphases. In addition, they differ as regards their internal ethos, in the ways that they are managed, in their sources of income, and to a greater or lesser extent in the socio-economic background of their students. Many secondary schools are *de facto* selective and about 10 per cent still charge fees.

At the end of the lower secondary cycle students take the Intermediate Certificate or the Group Certificate. At the end of the upper secondary cycle they take the Leaving Certificate.

Special education

Mentally handicapped children are educated in special schools or in special classes attached to local schools. While special provision exists for physically handicapped children, they are educated as far as possible in normal schools.

Private education

Less than 4 per cent of all primary schools are "non-aided", that is, are strictly private and entirely self-financing. It should be noted, however, that some of the private secondary schools are among the most prestigious in the land. Apart from boarding establishments, most "non-aided" schools are located in the main towns and cities.

Post-secondary education

In Ireland, post-secondary education is normally termed "third-level". Historically, there have been nominally only two autonomous universities, the National University of Ireland and Dublin University, more familiarly known as Trinity College. The former comprises the three colleges of Dublin, Cork and Galway, together with St. Patrick's, Maynooth, which has a special affiliated status. In effect, there have been the equivalent of five university establishments since the constituents of the National University are no less independent than many institutions designated as universities in other countries.

A Higher Education Authority was established on an *ad hoc* basis in 1968 and instituted in 1971 as a statutory body charged with allocating the State's block grant to the universities, forward planning, and advising the Minister of Education on emerging higher education needs.

In 1989, after the examiners' visit the Government announced that the two National Institutes of Higher Education in Dublin and Limerick were to become universities. This means that Ireland will soon have *four* universities officially, and in practice seven university-level establishments.

Other third-level (tertiary) institutions comprise: nine regional colleges; vocational colleges in Dublin and Limerick; the National College of Arts and Design; six teacher training colleges. Some of these institutions are affiliated to a university.

As in other OECD countries, enrolments in post-secondary education have increased steadily, from 20 700 in 1965/66 to 25 000 in 1970/71, to 41 500 in 1980/81, and to 67 375 in 1984-85. This is still not a high proportion of those eligible for admission (Diagram 3). Much of the expansion has taken place outside the universities and teacher training colleges; the latter, as will be seen in Chapter 6, have recently suffered a sharp numerical decline. The official policy has been to create and develop, as rapidly as possible, institutions capable of producing graduates qualified as high-level technicians or as specialists in new or expanding occupational fields.

Training

Separate from the formal education system are the quasi-independent governmental agencies responsible for training; FAS, the industrial training and employment agency; CERT, the hotel, catering and tourism training authority; TEAGASC, the advisory and training agency of the agricultural and food industries. Each of these is governed by a board comprising representatives of industry, employers, trade unions, government, and independent interests. They are strictly employment-oriented, striving to adapt programmes to changing market demands. Their services are equally open to adults but most of their clients are young people.

FAS functions include the provision of employment programmes, the provision of post-school placement and guidance services and support for co-operative and community-based enterprise.

The school training division of CERT has responsibility for the recruitment of school-leavers for formal training at hotel and catering colleges, the development of training courses and national certification, and placement of students for periods of industrial experience during training.

Of particular importance in TEAGASC's remit is education and training for young farmers, research in the food industry, together with farm management, economics, marketing of agricultural products and rural development.

Diagram 3. **COMPARISON BETWEEN THE PROPORTION OF AN AGE GROUP OBTAINING A SECOND LEVEL - SECOND STAGE QUALIFICATION ALLOWING ACCESS TO THIRD LEVEL EDUCATION AND THE PROPORTION ACTUALLY ENROLLING 1985-86**

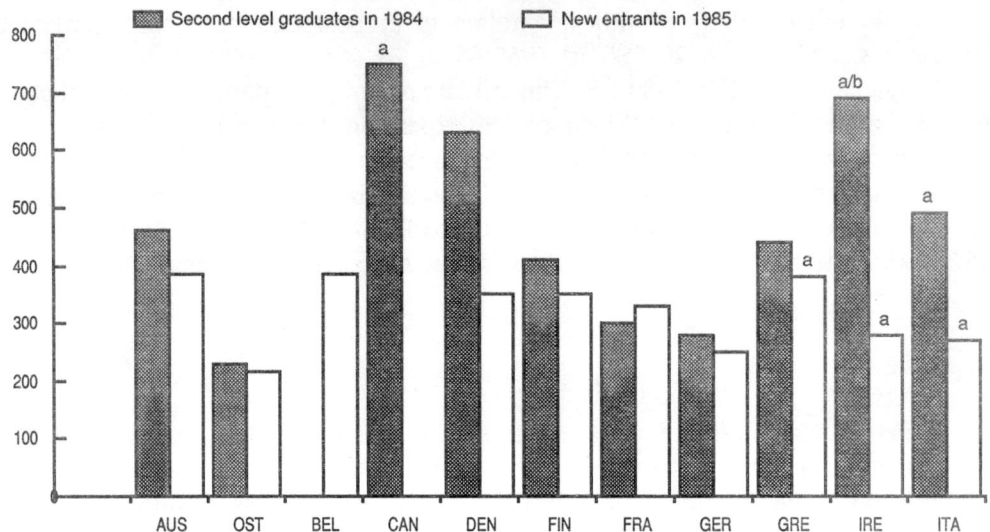

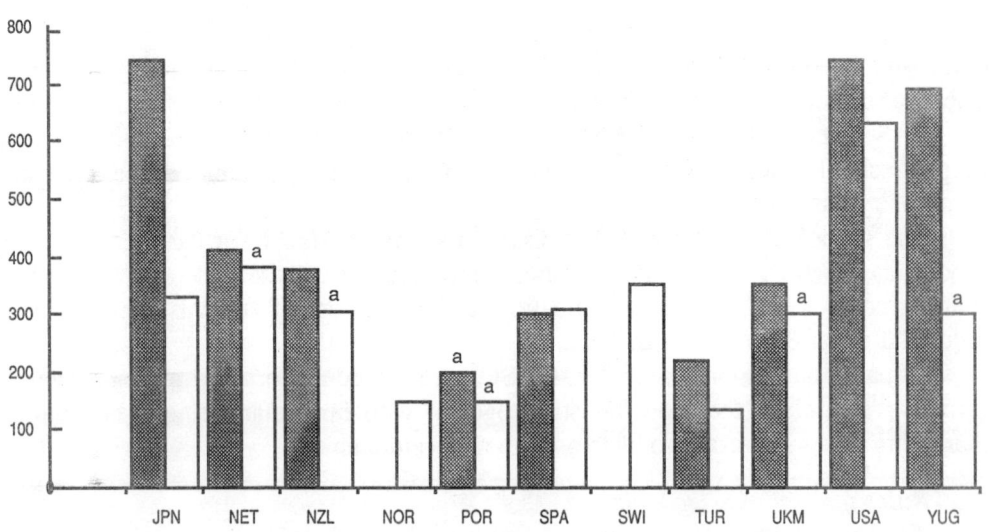

a) 1984-85.
b) Number of pupils attending the terminal examination.
Source: "Education in OECD Countries 1985-86: Comparative Statistics", OECD, Paris, 1988 (General Distribution).

Adult education

Adult education is provided by the universities, other post-secondary institutions, Vocational Education Committees, community and comprehensive schools, some secondary schools, various other institutions and a number of voluntary institutions. Most of the public provision is offered by the Vocational Education Committees. Nearly all programmes are provided on a part-time basis. There has been much reference to the ideal of lifelong learning and the importance of second-chance education, notably in the *Report of the Commission on Adult Education* but, as in nearly all other countries, there is no evidence of any concerted effort to render it a reality.

NOTES AND REFERENCES

1. In Ireland, it is customary to refer to first-level, second-level and third-level education and to the junior and senior cycle of secondary education. The term "primary" is also used so as to comprehend both pre-primary or early schooling. In this report it is proposed to use the OECD terminology of pre-primary, primary, lower secondary, upper secondary, and post-secondary education.
2. *Cf.* Hyland, A., and Milne, K., *Irish Educational Documents*, Vol. 1 (Dublin, 1987), p. 62. A parliamentary bill for the improvement of the education of the lower orders of people in the kingdom in 1799 contained the following proposal: "That one or more schools with a house for the master, or mistress thereof may be erected...in every parish or union of parishes in this kingdom for the education of children in such parish or union in reading, writing, arithmetic, mensuration, and such other things as may be suited to their several destinations and capacities; and for the instruction of the said children in husbandry, gardening, planting; in plainwork, knitting, weaving of lace, and other useful occupations, according to their different sexes, and ages."
3. *Cf. Submissions*, p. 483.
4. *Rules for National Schools.*
5. According to the Irish designation there are 581 000 pupils in primary schools but 140 000 of these are in pre-primary or infant classes.
6. *Rules for National Schools* - Rule 68.

Chapter 3

ISSUES AND PROBLEMS

Expansion and its aftermath

The system of education in Ireland has been under fierce pressure throughout the past thirty years. It has been obliged to find places in the primary and secondary sectors at a speed and on a scale experienced by few other OECD countries. It has had to develop post-school education and training provision almost from scratch. It has had to meet a large demand for places in universities while constructing a non-university post-school sector designed expressly to train young people for the needs of a modernising economy. It has had to invest heavily in new buildings and extra staff at all levels. It has had to manage this quantitative expansion and considerable qualitative improvement while respecting the sensitivities of powerful interest groups and avoiding any root-and-branch reforms of structures or brusque changes of direction. It has also had to make do with fewer resources than many other countries have had the good fortune to command. At the present time, the resource constraints are as tight as they have ever been.

The remarkable thing is that there has been relatively little conflict and there have been few signs of public dissatisfaction, at least until very recently. Morale has remained steady. Has not "Education for the Irish... always been held in high esteem"?[1] Most Irish people, in and out of the education system, take pride in the conviction that they have one of the best educated younger generations in the world. Everyone speaks of the excellent quality of the teaching force and the respected status of teachers in society. But there are urgent issues and problems that must be confronted and there are policy priorities to be determined. Some issues have already surfaced; others are beginning to emerge; a few are perhaps only appropriate for disinterested outsiders to raise.

Forces for change

Some educators in Ireland are persuaded that there have been sweeping reforms in the education system since the first OECD educational policy review. The truth is that, although there has certainly been the remarkable quantitative expansion and creation of new types of secondary school just described and although there have been several important curricular developments, the system as such has remained largely the same. Like the majority of education systems it is of its nature conservative and slow to change; it has behaved reactively rather than pro-actively. Official and other reports, while acknowledging the achievements of the system despite limited resources, have reiterated the necessity of improving classroom organisation, equipment and materials, teaching methods, and learning outcomes.

Forces are now in operation, however, that are bound to have far-reaching consequences. One such force is the demographic downturn. Another is the inexorable withdrawal of the religious orders from control and management of secondary schools. It is proposed, in this chapter, to discuss these and other forces with a view to explaining the background against which the condition of teaching and teachers, now and in the future, is to be understood.

The discussion is arranged under five headings: *i)* the overall context of control and management; *ii)* policy- and decision-making and planning, *iii)* research and development; *iv)* role of the inspectorate; *v)* financing and scarce resources.

Control and management of a patchwork system

The first point to be made about the Irish education system is that it is difficult to understand. Professional educators confess that even the vocabulary and acronyms used to describe its various structural parts and its processes are baffling to the outsider. Although a small system, it has the same administrative apparatus and faces the same problems of control, management, and monitoring as large systems, besides problems of its own making. The schools are locally managed to an unusual degree but in so far as the exercise of its specific powers are concerned, the Department of Education functions like a classic, highly centralised bureaucracy. The system appears on the surface to be privatised to an extraordinary degree but is predominantly a public service. By the same token, the Catholic Church appears to wield immense influence.

The seeming paradoxes and complexity derive from the way the system has evolved over a long time. It was not planned methodically but expanded in piecemeal fashion in order to respond to importunate pressures. There have been no grand designs in the classic mode of centralised government. Under English rule, education for Catholics, the vast majority of the population, was provided under the aegis of the Church. Broadly speaking, primary schools were managed by parish priests under the overall surveillance of the diocesan bishops while the religious orders ran the secondary schools. Resources were always exiguous. After independence, management remained in the hands of the Church while the State assumed the lion's share of financial responsibility and only actively intervened to fill perceived gaps and satisfy new social and economic demands.

Since the early 1960s the scale of state intervention has significantly increased as new demands have intensified. The Church, for its part, because of the drastic fall in the number of religious resulting from the decline in vocations, recognises that it cannot continue to play its historic role as the *principal* actor. It remains, however, a *major* actor on the educational stage, as it does in all aspects of the Irish social system. Ireland has arrived at a watershed in its educational history when the control and management of institutions as well as their financing are being progressively and ineluctably secularised. However, secularisation is unlikely ever to be total or to lead to uniformity given that Ireland appears to be irrevocably wedded to the idea of local and independent management of schools.

To a rare extent among OECD countries, schools appear to be under private control. The State owns relatively few educational institutions. The system is commonly described as an *aided* one, with the State assisting non-governmental bodies to provide education at all levels. But, in practice, there is not a private monopoly since the government exercises substantial powers. By far the greater part of educational financing is voted by Parliament and allocated by the Minister of Education through the Department of Education. Building policy is *de facto* in the Minister's hands. Teachers' salaries and other essential expenditures are paid in full and directly by the Department, except in the case of the private secondary schools which distribute the E44 (administrative term) "basic" salary to teachers. Schools which do not charge fees are reimbursed for this "basic" salary but the fact that the secondary authorities pay the "basic" emphasizes that they are the employers of the teachers. In order to qualify for support, schools must satisfy prescribed criteria concerning their management, staffing, organisation and physical facilities. The critical measure of pupil/teacher ratios is fixed by the Minister. The Department determines the curriculum and teachers' qualifications, employs an inspectorate to monitor standards, and establishes rules for the management and physical maintenance of schools. The primary schools have always been better known as *national* schools and organised as a *public* service.

In short, schools are controlled by a partnership or duumvirate of the State and local managers. It is a collaborative arrangement that arose and that has been conserved through force of circumstance. Yet it means that Ireland has already in place that close relationship between the central administration and local institutions to which many countries now aspire. The flaw is that the relationship has not so far made for dynamic movement for reasons that will now be considered.

Policy- and decision-making, and planning

Besides innate conservatism there are three constraints on the system that inhibit change: *i)* the absence, certainly until relatively recently, of a purposeful central authority having the political will, administrative capacity, and requisite financial resources to formulate and implement reforms; *ii)* the presence of powerful interest groups outside government; *iii)* the intrinsic complexity of the system that has already been mentioned.

Consider, first, the limitations upon the freedom of manoeuvre of the Minister of Education. According to the Constitution the Minister is entirely responsible for the policies, administration and day-to-day functioning of the Department of Education. That singular responsibility is at once a stern reality and a mixed blessing, for it makes the Minister accountable to the *Dail Eireann*, the national parliament, and the Dail is notoriously quick to raise awkward questions and issues. The consequence of this is that civil servants are conditioned to err on the side of caution, and Ministers wish to avoid becoming embroiled in sensitive conflicts likely to attract adverse publicity.

The freedom of the Minister is further circumscribed by the regular process of overall government decision-making. Vital decisions affecting education are negotiated among several ministries, including the Department of Finance, which has notable clout. The negotiating process is often protracted and may result in outcomes not necessarily desired by the Minister or the Department.

The tendency to be cautious and circumspect politically is reinforced by the necessity of temporising with non-governmental interest groups ensconced in redoubtable positions. Besides the Catholic Church, other groups also have to be reckoned with, notably the Vocational Education Committees in the regions and the very active and well organised professional teacher associations with their formidable negotiating skills. The examiners heard frequent allusions to teacher unions as a power bloc.

It is, however, the relationship between State and Church that remains the most intriguing factor for the external observer. As explained above, the State exercises a much tighter grip on education than appears at first sight. The fact remains that the State would not contemplate subverting the authority of the Church in educational matters either by usurping any of its functions or by introducing measures that it would be likely to find unpalatable. Change is only feasible through discreet negotiations and an unspoken search for consensus. In this connection, it is vital to record that it is not a question of the Church being against change while the State is all for it. For one thing the Church, although playing a leading role, is not monolithic. On the contrary, there have always been tensions between the bishops and religious orders about how secondary schools should be managed and organised, and there have always been differences of approach and style among the religious orders. Some members of the Church hold advanced and even radical educational ideas, and many of its schools and colleges are always ready to experiment and innovate. It is rather a question of the State not embarking on a reform affecting the school system as a whole without the implicit or explicit assent of the Church and, where applicable, other interest groups.

The third factor is the very patchwork of structures and processes already described. The tidy-minded or authoritarian politician would itch to rationalise the overall system or at least major parts of it. No Minister of Education in Ireland could be committed to such folly. The complexity and plurality, the very ambiguity, are taken for granted.

In addition to these constraints on the freedom of action of the Minister of Education, three further features merit comment. First, most ministers have held office for too short a time to grow into the post, let alone to initiate long-term strategic plans. The short duration of many appointments used to be compounded by the fact that the portfolio was considered neither prestigious nor demanding. The statement made by one minister in 1956 has been frequently cited. It was not his duty, he declared, "to philosophise on educational matters" but to act like "a kind of dungaree man, the plumber who will make the satisfactory communications and streamline the forces and potentialities of the educational workers and educational management in this country"[2]. Over the past three decades, however, several outstanding politicians have occupied the post and given it greatly enhanced status. Moreover, ministers have recently been kept in office for longer periods of time. Conditions are thus much more favourable than in the past for thinking through and initiating positive policies.

Secondly, no minister in an Irish government can afford to neglect the constituents who have elected him or her to the *Dail*. If this ensures that a Minister of Education is in permanent contact with grass-roots opinion and is therefore more aware of micro needs and issues than most OECD Ministers of Education, it also encroaches on the time available for policy formulation and overseeing the work of the Department of Education.

The third feature meriting attention is the lack of sophisticated machinery for providing the minister with comprehensive and authoritative information and advice. Up to a point the permanent officials of the Department of Education, headed by the Secretary, are there to collect evidence and tender advice. However, as will be seen, the Department is over-stretched simply to administer the education system. Furthermore, it is neither conditioned nor appropriately equipped to advise systematically on policy.

More recently, incoming ministers have appointed a personal adviser or assistant who can be relied upon to seek information as required, to liaise with civil servants and external agencies on the minister's behalf, and to have an eye on the minister's public relations. This is evidently a constructive development. It may be argued, however, that the minister still requires considerably more support than that in the shape of data gathering and forward planning. This could entail, *inter alia*, the setting up of a small cabinet, which, admittedly, might have cost implications, the creation of a strategic planning unit within the Department of Education by means of some degree of internal reorganisation, the appointment of a national advisory body, and the calculated use of the inspectorate as a source of innovative ideas and an engine of change. A more detailed discussion of possibilities would take us beyond the scope of the present review.

Following the OECD review of the mid-1960s which highlighted the paucity of data on which to debate educational matters and plan for the future, a planning and development unit was established within the Department of Education but later abolished in 1973. A Council of Education had been established in 1950. The Minister of Education requested it to report on the curricula of primary and secondary schools. Its two reports of 1954 and 1962 were generally perceived as very conservative and it was allowed to wither away. The inspectorate has been used occasionally and haphazardly as a source of intelligence but that is not seen as one of its regular functions. It is almost as though there has been in-built resistance to creating any permanent machinery for facilitating the policy-making process. This was to be expected so long as the Minister of Education played a detached role but has become surprising as the State has assumed the leading role in education and ministers have found themselves much more exposed to criticism in the *Dail* and by public opinion. The establishment of the Curriculum and Examination Board in 1984 and of its successor, the National Council for Curriculum and Assessment in 1987, reflects a new awareness of the desirability of establishing a semi-independent advisory body, at least for curricular and assessment purposes.

The Department of Education

The present position of the Department of Education is unenviable. On the one hand, it is criticised by certain educators for intervening either too much or too little according to their point of view. On the other hand, its initiating and discretionary powers are circumscribed as compared with those of certain other ministries of education in OECD countries, and it operates with conspicuously scarce human and material resources. It is, constitutionally, the handmaiden of the minister, but is quite often blamed for governmental or ministerial decisions over which it has had little influence.

Like that of the minister, its profile has been greatly heightened over the past three decades. The general impression in the education field is that it displayed notable creativity, energy and purpose from about 1965 until the end of the 1970s, but that in more recent years it has shown signs of being extenuated by an oppressive workload and the stress of allocating diminishing financial resources.

The Department is not under strain because of any attempt to over-reach its powers. On the contrary, despite the masterly inactivity of ministers in the past and their frequently short tenure of office, it seldom sought to acquire a policy-making or even a major advisory role. The main reason for this is that it has never questioned the doctrine of ministerial responsibility. A second and related reason is that it is not oriented towards change. It perceives its task as that of interpreting the prescribed rules and regulations and administering the system as it is rather than of initiating change. In any case, its administrative task is so exacting as to leave small room for other activities. Because there are no local authorities other than the Vocational Education Committees, the Department deals directly with individual educational establishments. It is thus concerned with nuts and bolts as well as with allocating major items of expenditure. On their own itinerary through Ireland the examiners encountered several times school principals who mentioned having discussed only recently with a ministry official permission to incur this or that small item of expenditure. In that connection it must be said that the relationship was invariably viewed as entirely cordial and the emphasis was on flexibility rather than obstruction.

The Department is concerned with such minor matters because there is no administrative layer interposed between it and individual institutions. The question arises, therefore, whether it would not be desirable to devolve some of the Department's routine functions to regionally based administrative units. This could serve the double purpose of improving overall efficiency and freeing the Department to address substantive matters designed to serve ministers in the development and implementation of policies.

The ready objection to devolution in the Irish context is that the country has a small population inhabiting a small geographic area, that the Department of Education has established over the years intimate contacts with local interests and institutions and that, therefore, to add another administrative level is quite superfluous. This is to overlook the fact that there remain distinctive regions in Ireland because of the strength of local tradition. There are also already in place regionally based authorities in the form of the Vocational Education Committees and regionally based teaching resource centres, which could be incorporated into larger entities. More importantly, recent international experience has revealed the importance of central authorities being sensitive to local area needs, and the advantage of co-ordinating and managing education and training as near to the level of self-contained regions as possible. As argued below, there is also the necessity of co-ordinating secondary school provision to better purpose.

The case for devolution with respect to the functioning of the Department is also worth considering. Having shed what amount to largely managerial functions, it could then concentrate on higher-level administration and policy-oriented tasks. That is a measure that has been adopted in several OECD countries in recent years.

We have so far discussed the role and functioning of the Department of Education within the framework of its own existing sphere of action and responsibility. It is to be noted that there is a general effort underway in Ireland to rationalise and streamline all sectors of public administration. Given this reforming context, our suggestions are not untimely. In particular, as we shall argue later on, there appears to be a powerful case on educational as well as overall efficiency grounds for much closer co-ordination of all education and training activities across administrative and executive boundaries both at the national and regional levels.

Research and development

Once again it is necessary to contrast the situation before the *Investment in Education* report and the situation that evolved thereafter. Before the mid-1960s the volume of educational research was minuscule and unconnected with any notion of development. Today, the study of education is well developed and it is possible to point to the existence of a reputable body of research, even when leaving on one side the steady flow of dissertations and theses being produced by post-graduate students. Ireland has now an Educational Studies Association and three research journals -- *Irish Educational Studies, Studies in Education and the Irish Journal of Education* -- which not only reveal evidence of much internal activity but of a close acquaintance with international research literature, particularly the large quantity emanating from the United States. In addition, there is one purpose-designed research centre at St. Patrick's Training College. Finally, some of the valuable studies of the national Economic and Social Research Institute deal directly or indirectly with matters of educational concern.

Although the universities and teacher training colleges complain that they are starved of funds for educational research, and although there have been relatively few empirical studies, the current overall output of pedagogically oriented research is impressive for a small country. Moreover, an attempt has been made to develop the curriculum using action research through pilot projects and experiments. What might be regarded as unsatisfactory is the dearth of policy-related research, as distinct from a growing body of policy discussion literature, especially in view of the fact that the investment-in-education exercise cast Ireland in the role of an international pioneer and seemed to promise a future in which research *and active development* would be treated as a high priority. Is it that the authorities in Ireland, like those in several OECD countries, have become disenchanted with the whole process of educational planning and, perhaps, dubious of the utility of the research findings brought to their attention, or is it that they have difficulty in identifying clear-cut priorities? Or does the daily pressure of their jobs preclude a systematic review of literature on policy issues?

The authors of *Investment in Education* recorded that: "One of the difficulties that confronted [them] at the beginning of the survey was the inadequacy of the educational statistics available"[3]. They themselves made up for the deficiency to an extraordinary degree. If the statistics available today are far superior to those available at the beginning of the 1960s they are not as wide-ranging or thorough as those compiled by the "Investment" team. Basic data and information on the functioning of the system are not always available in sufficient scope or in good time. Statistical reports appear late and their figures do not always illuminate current issues. The examiners were told by several of their interlocutors that it was difficult to form a coherent picture of the regulations, as there was no up-to-date or compendious version accumulated year after year. Since 1964 the Department has not issued an annual report. The reports on schools by inspectors are not published as a rule, although it is generally believed that they contain valuable information that could be regularly summarised for the benefit of all those involved directly and indirectly in the management of schools. All this prompts the question, foreshadowed above, whether the minister can turn to a sufficiently strong body of quantitative and qualitative data on which to base policy judgements and whether such data should not be accessible to all those with a major interest in education.

Role of the Inspectorate

There are two inspectorates, one for the primary and one for the secondary sector. Although having a common head, the Chief Inspector, they function as two separate entities. Both are generally recognised to be chronically under-staffed in relation to the scope of their duties. There are few women among their ranks. In a cross-national perspective their role may be summed up as *sui generis*.

The primary inspectors are charged, mainly and unequivocally, with the task of evaluating the performance of schools and appraising the competence of teachers. Many are located at the regional level. The examiners ascertained that, despite their small numbers, they are frequent visitors to schools, which see them as emissaries of the Department of Education and hold them in evident respect not too far removed from deference. Primary inspectors are also assigned specific responsibilities, some minor and others major, including the comprehensive reform of the school curriculum and organising in-service courses for teachers.

The secondary inspectors visit schools very rarely and though having the functions of appraisal do not exercise them. Much of their time and most of their resources are concentrated on administering and supervising national examinations.

The inspectors are not autonomous but civil servants employed by the Department of Education, even being sometimes described as "outdoors staff". They do not undertake independent initiatives. Their reports are not published and are mediated by the Department. All this might be regarded as surprising in view of the fact that they are nearly all recruited from the teaching force and collectively constitute a formidable body of professional expertise. It is not that their expertise is being totally squandered;

on the contrary, they are making a valuable contribution to Irish education. It is rather that their full potential is far from being tapped.

Of late, several OECD countries have been reappraising the role of their educational inspectorates, against the background of public debates about standards, quality in schools, and a demand for greater accountability. An alternative model of functions and organisation, on which Ireland might wish to ponder, is to create a unified primary/secondary inspectorate with quasi-autonomous status, which, while evaluating the performance of individual schools, serves as the eyes and ears of the Minister of Education, and plays a major part in disseminating information and stimulating innovative experiments. In the Irish context, that would entail the shedding of certain existing duties. In-service training courses, for example, as suggested below, might well be arranged by teacher training centres, colleges of education, and university education departments in regular consultation with the inspectorate. The question of setting and administering examinations is also pertinent (see Chapter 5).

In passing, it is perhaps worth considering the question of in-service training for inspectors themselves. What arrangements are in place for ensuring that inspectors remain up-to-date and professionally competent in their several duties? In the perspective of the single European market will they have opportunities to go abroad and to exchange experiences with foreign colleagues?

A more important question concerns the overall evaluation of the school system. Inspectors' reports on individual schools are no doubt valuable, though some critics allege that they are much too subjective. They are not a substitute for a sophisticated continuing review of what is happening inside the entire education system.

If it is recognised that the inspectors are an indispensable link between schools and the Department, their numbers should necessarily expand and their functions should diversify in step with the quantitative and qualitative growth of the education system. In recent years, it is the reverse trend that has prevailed. The inspectorate has become under-resourced and under-staffed. The consequence has been less quality control and a weakening contribution to the overall accountability of the system. At the same time, because of a lack of development of teacher and school self-evaluation at the periphery and the inadequate data collection and analysis at the centre, it has not been possible to compensate for the inadequacy of the inspectorate presence.

There is, accordingly, a need for rethinking the role and specific tasks of the inspectorate in the context of the major changes that will be affecting the education system during the next ten years. The authorities will have to choose between an inspectorate of the present size or an enlarged one. The first option would imply a reduction of its present tasks and concentration on auditing school performance and reporting to and advising the Minister and the Department. If the second option were to be adopted, its multiple tasks would call for a diversified staff, grouped in specialised, horizontal units, and strong central leadership. The examiners believe that the system could only benefit from having an enlarged, unified and more independent inspectorate with clearly defined functions.

Financing and scarce resources

At several points we have emphasized that the Irish education system has always had to make do with scarce resources. There are two fundamental explanations for this austerity:

i) The high birth rate over time and consequential heavy demand for school places: in the past at the compulsory level, more recently at the upper secondary level as well;

ii) The fact that Ireland has been, and remains, a relatively poor country.

The paucity of resources has been compounded by the historic assumption that the proprietors of schools would contribute significantly to overall costs and that the State's financial commitment was not absolute, by the woefully inadequate infrastructure and old building stock inherited in 1922, and by the uneconomic geographical distribution of schools graphically illustrated in *Investment in Education*.

Today, many school proprietors still make an important contribution towards overall costs, frequently in the form of the foregone earnings of some teaching staff and the unpaid secretarial, cleaning and caretaking work of members of religious communities. This contribution is diminishing, however, and will eventually cease to be significant. As things are, many Irish schools appear spartan and short of space compared with schools in many other OECD countries. Many classes are still large despite a sustained effort to reduce class size between 1973 and 1986. There are shortages of ordinary teaching and learning aids, special equipment, laboratories, libraries, new instructional technology, and recreational areas. Few non-teaching staff -- caretakers, cleaners and secretaries -- are employed. Many principals have no secretarial help. At the same time, the numerous schools constructed since the early 1960s are functionally efficient and aesthetically pleasing. It is also clear that some schools are receiving substantial financial and other assistance from parents. By comparative standards it can be argued, indeed, that the Irish education system is very productive because it achieves so much with substantially fewer publicly-provided resources than most OECD countries.

The system might have been in a less straitened condition had the social demand for upper and post-secondary education since the 1960s been resisted and had the salaries of teachers been depressed. In the event, no brake was put on secondary school or post-secondary expansion, at least until recently, and teachers have been receiving good salaries. Moreover, it has been necessary since the mid-1970s to devote increasingly large resources to combating youth unemployment by means of education and training programmes, among other measures (Table 5 shows expenditure on labour-market programmes not too far short of that on education).

Table 5. **Public expenditure on labour market programmes in 1985-1988 as a percentage of GDP**

	1985	1986	1987	1988
		Ireland		
Employment services and administration	0.15	0.15	0.17	0.15
Labour market training (adults)	0.66	0.60	0.55	0.52
Special youth measures	0.47	0.44	0.50	0.43
Direct job creation and employment subsidies	0.18	0.33	0.32	0.30
Measures for the disabled	–	–	–	–
Subtotal: "active" measures	**1.46**	**1.52**	**1.54**	**1.40**
Unemployment compensation	3.72	3.76	3.62	3.42
Early retirement for labour market reasons	–	–	–	–
Subtotal: Income maintenance	**3.72**	**3.76**	**3.62**	**3.42**
Grand total	5.18	5.28	5.16	4.83

Source: OECD Employment Outlook 1989, OECD, Paris, p. 206.

The charge certainly cannot be levelled against Ireland that it has sold education short in recent times. Between 1961/62 and 1986 expenditure on education as a percentage of GNP more than doubled from 2.83 to 6.60 per cent. As a percentage of public service spending that expenditure rose from 13.87 per cent in 1961/62 to 18.51 per cent in 1988. The Background Report points out that although government spending generally rose sharply as a percentage of Gross National Product over the period 1961/62 to 1987/88, spending on education rose more quickly[4]. Diagram 4 and Table 6 show that public expenditure on education as a percentage of GDP was around the average for OECD countries in 1985. Table 7 shows that expenditure as a percentage of total public spending was somewhat below the average.

But, of course, in order to provide the same variety and intensity of educational services as most other OECD countries, Ireland would have had to devote a much higher percentage of its GDP and its public expenditure to education simply because it was catering for far greater numbers. Table 8 shows that in 1985 only Greece spent less on other expenditures than teachers' salaries. We were informed that 92 per cent of expenditure on primary schools and more than 70 per cent on secondary schools go

Diagram 4. **PERCENTAGE OF GDP DEVOTED TO PUBLIC EXPENDITURE ON EDUCATION 1985-86**

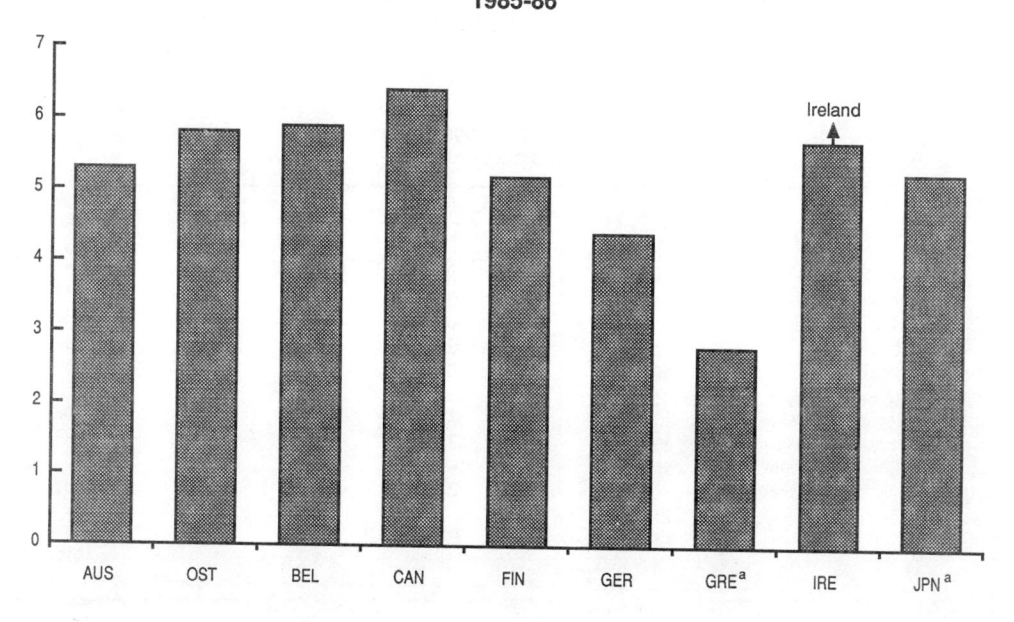

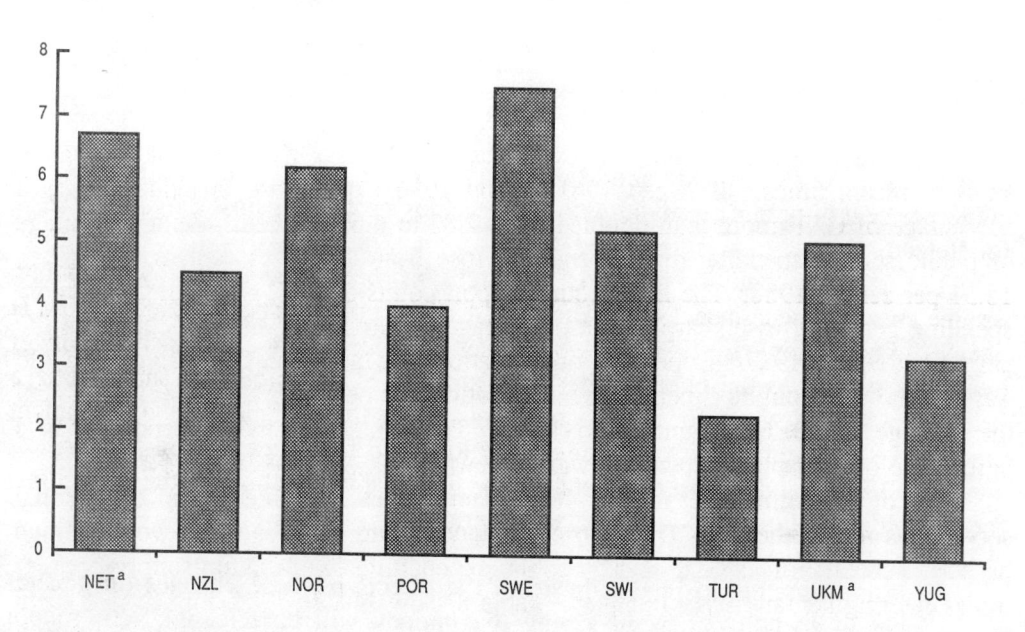

a) 1984.
Source: "Education in OECD Countries 1985-86: Comparative Statistics", OECD, Paris, 1988 (General Distribution).

Table 6. **Total expenditure[a] on education (by sources) in 1985**
In local currency and at current prices

Country	Public sources (millions)	Private sources (millions)	Percentage of GDP Public sources	Percentage of GDP Private sources	Total
Australia	12 925.0	866.9	5.38	0.36	5.74
Austria	78 638.6	..	5.81	..	..
Belgium	287 387.7	..	5.93	..	..
Canada	30 287.1	2 787.0	6.37	0.59	6.95
Finland	17 682.1	1 194.9	5.25	0.35	5.60
France[b]	257 088.0	46 458.0	5.93	1.08	7.01
Germany	80 786.0	2 904.0	4.41	0.16	4.57
Greece[b]	100 293.5	9 031.4	2.64	0.24	2.88
Ireland	**996.2**	**48.9**	**5.75**	**0.23**	**6.21**
Japan[b]	15 665 383.0	4 017 652.0	5.26	1.35	6.61
Netherlands[b]	26 644.0	731.0	6.66	0.18	6.84
New Zealand	2 028.4	..	4.52	..	..
Norway	30 956.0	724.0	6.17	0.14	6.31
Portugal	140 637.9	..	3.99	..	..
Sweden	65 000.6	..	7.55	..	..
Switzerland	11 696.3	240.2	5.13	0.11	5.13
Turkey	627 104.0	..	2.28	..	..
United Kingdom[b]	16 678.3	..	5.23	..	..
Yugoslavia	386 936.3	..	3.24	–	3.24

a) Including transactions relating to loans for Austria, Germany, Ireland, the Netherlands, Norway, Sweden, Switzerland and Yugoslavia.
b) 1984.
Source: "Education in OECD Countries 1985-86: Comparative Statistics", OECD, Paris, 1988 (General Distribution).

to salaries. New Zealand, another country with a small population, allocated 46.48 per cent of public expenditure to non-teaching costs as against a figure of 22.19 for Ireland.

The endemic condition of scarce resources has been exacerbated by the public service cuts imposed since 1986. The pupil/teacher ratio has been increased, but is planned to come down by 1990/91 (see Chapter 6). Vice-principal posts are no longer treated as surplus to the pupil/teacher ratio and this is tantamount to suppressing a teaching post. Vacances for inspectors are not being filled. Science and equipment grants have been reduced. A system already lean is being squeezed still further.

The Background Report comments on the financial implications of the projections for declining enrolments in sagely guarded terms:

"It is not possible to predict in detail the effects of these changes on general education spending, beyond saying that money will be released from school building, general recurrent expenditure, and teachers' salaries for use either *elsewhere in education or elsewhere in total government spending*".

Table 7. **Public expenditure on education**[a] **(including subsidies) in 1985**
In local currency and at current prices

Country	Current expenditure (millions)	Capital expenditure (millions)	Total (millions)	Total as % of total public expenditure	Total public expenditure as % of GDP
Australia	13 110.0	1 143.0	14 254.0	15.42	38.50
Austria	70 846.5	7 189.5	78 638.6	10.57	54.93
Belgium[b]	272 843.0	14 544.7	287 387.7	10.93	53.90
Canada[c]	30 176.0	2 253.0	32 429.0	14.43	47.23
Finland	17 604.2	1 362.5	18 966.7	13.61	41.36
France[d]	244 704.0	14 176.0	258 880.0	11.46	52.74
Germany[b]	75 566.0	6 252.0	83 690.0	9.63	47.45
Greece[d]	96 314.8	3 955.5	100 293.5	6.56	40.20
Ireland	**901.5**	**94.9**	**996.2**	**10.61**	**53.92**
Japan[d]	..	..	15 665 383.1	15.83	33.21
Netherlands[d]	24 168.0	1 415.0	27 375.0	11.22	60.96
New Zealand	1 849.0	179.4	2 028.4	10.12[e]	..
Norway	27 979.0	1 580.0	31 680.0	13.23	..
Portugal	125 489.3	15 273.6	140 762.9	..	47.70
Sweden	57 702.7	3 024.8	65 000.6	11.68	64.63
Switzerland	10 738.4	1 039.0	11 696.3	16.55	31.01
Turkey	523 102.0	104 002.0	627 104.0	..	..
United Kingdom[d]	16 007.5	670.8	16 678.3	10.90	47.96
Yugoslavia	391 344.6	19 083.6	419 798.2	..	..

a) Including transactions relating to loans for Austria, Germany, Ireland, the Netherlands, Norway, Sweden, Switzerland and Yugoslavia.
b) Expenditure of the Ministries of Education only; in percentage of central government expenditure.
c) Including private expenditure on public education.
d) 1984.
e) Total public and private expenditure.
Source: "Education in OECD Countries 1985-86: Comparative Statistics", OECD, Paris, 1988 (General Distribution).

We have italicised the critical phrase. Since it is hard to see how educational expenditure as a percentage of GNP or of public expenditure could be increased without some unlikely trade-off -- there are already many more claims on the public purse than it can possibly satisfy -- the only two potential sources of revenue for relieving the present financial siege and initiating qualitative improvements are:

  i) a share of the increasing GNP, referred to in Chapter 1;
  ii) the savings accruing from declining enrolments.

In Chapter 1 the examiners expressed their understanding that Ireland is determined to have a well-educated, productive, and inventive population prepared for full economic participation in the greater European Community. Given its relatively poor economy, the burden of attaining that goal falls heavily on the nation's schools. Today, the typical job in an advanced industrialised society demands a level of functional literacy

Table 8. **Current expenditure on public education[a] by purpose, in 1985**
Percentage breakdown

Country	Administration	Emoluments Total	Of which: of teaching staff	School books	Scholarships	Welfare services	Other non-distributed[b]
Australia[c]	[d]	[d]	[d]	[d]	4.88	2.17	92.95
Austria	14.32	64.38	49.85	1.27	2.97	1.07	16.00
Belgium	0.84	77.60	..	0.04	..	1.68	14.41
Canada[e]	2.38	68.95	51.63	7.02	4.37	4.29	12.99
Finland[e]	2.26	64.79	47.58	6.94	4.62	8.52	12.88
France[f]	0.77	74.55	..	2.10	1.94	10.09	10.55
Germany[e]	1.22	78.11	..	..	1.14	2.89	16.66
Greece[f]	..	91.88	85.01	..	0.17	1.03	6.92
Ireland	**1.46**	**80.76**	**77.81**	**0.25**	**1.88**	**4.42**	**18.04**
Japan[g]	..	65.56	52.44	..	..	..	34.44
Netherlands[f]	1.32	68.43	66.78	4.07	5.22	1.87	19.10
New Zealand	0.04	67.10	53.52	20.75	4.62	2.71	4.78
Norway	2.98	67.61	..	6.59	5.26	2.34	15.23
Portugal	3.03	83.88	..	..	..	3.11	9.98
Switzerland	..	80.68	66.45	3.32	1.99[b]	..	14.02
Turkey	11.46	79.25	..	0.48	..	4.55	4.26
United Kingdom[f]	..	61.79	49.89	3.99	8.00	4.87	21.35
Yugoslavia	..	62.53	..	8.27	1.38	8.97	18.84

a) For Belgium and the Netherlands current expenditure on public and private education.
b) Only Austria and Sweden have provided separate data for the item "non distributed" which amounts to 4.55 per cent of total current expenditure in the first case and to 21.26 per cent in the second.
c) 1984. Expenditure on school health services is covered by the Ministry of Health.
d) Included in "Other".
e) Public and private expenditure.
f) 1984.
g) 1984, public and private expenditure.
Source: "Education in OECD Countries 1985-86: Comparative Statistics", OECD, Paris, 1988 (General Distribution).

and an ability to be analytical that far exceeds the demands of many jobs even ten and twenty years ago. This places a premium on the very quality of the instruction offered in the schools. In our view, six sets of resources have a direct bearing on that quality: the teachers, the teacher training institutions, teachers' centres, the inspectorate, the school as a work place, and the Council for Curriculum and Assessment. In order to function effectively all require increased support. It is to be hoped, therefore, that education will benefit from the recent and continuing upturn in the economy and annual increases in the gross national product and from the savings due to arise from declining enrolments. Naturally, priorities will have to be determined, and the Department of Education will have to prepare its annual estimates imaginatively with continuing qualitative improvement over an extended time frame always in mind and yet a sharp eye for cost-effective criteria. We would only affirm that significant qualitative improvement over the next decade in the education of young people in Ireland must rely ultimately on changes in the behaviour of already trained teachers, the great majority of whom were educated themselves and professionally trained before the electronic revolution. This will entail a substantial financial outlay on *in-service training* and call for improved resources within the schools in order to enhance teacher effectiveness.

NOTES AND REFERENCES

1. *Submissions*, p. 335.
2. *Dail Debates*, Vol. 159, 19 July 1956.
3. *Investment in Education*, p. 3.
4. *Background Report*, p. 81.

Chapter 4

THE SCHOOLS: ORGANISATION AND PRACTICE

The responsiveness of the schools to social requirements

The first and most important question to address in considering the organisation and practice of schools in Ireland is their adequacy to meet the present and emerging educational needs of the country. This puts the matter in a perspective which is appropriate to an external review[1], even though it inevitably gives rise to a second question, namely, the actual and potential capability for change should it seem desirable. It is necessary to approach these two questions from an understanding of how the present organisation and practice of schooling have acquired their distinguishing features. This understanding, partial as it must be, conditions our comments and recommendations.

Schooling is not just so many pieces of machinery which can be assembled or dismantled and replaced according to changing circumstances. It has its own momentum and direction. The Irish experience in the past three decades, when many innovations have been attempted, demonstrates that structural, organisational and pedagogical reform requires careful, long-term planning, high-level negotiating skills, resource outlays, and a considerable measure of patience.

Consistent roles and functions of schools

Despite the variety of religious and secular authorities, and the differential impact of the secularisation factors identified in Chapter 3, the organisation of teaching and learning in primary and secondary schools seems highly consistent throughout the country. This consistency is not accidental and demonstrates the continuing weight of tradition and a tacit set of values and expectations regarding education. We have discussed this already in Chapter 1 and will return to it in Chapter 5. But the point bears reiteration, since it is necessary to appreciate the historical origins and early developments of schools within the two principal streams, primary (elementary) and post-primary, each of which achieved a distinctive and pervasive ethos according to the widespread educational and social norms of the epoch. In this respect, the general organisation of primary and secondary education in Ireland parallels that in most other OECD countries.

At the level of school organisation and pedagogical practice these elements may be summarised by reference to: the social sorting and selecting functions of schools; normative emphasis on conformity to rules and procedures (discipline); stratification of pupils according to social and psychological assumptions about human differences; a pedagogical mode which derives from long-established ideas about the ordering, segmentation and transmission of knowledge, and development of skills through supervised exercises and practice usually in individually managed (one teacher) formal classrooms, or, to a small degree, simulated real-life settings. Notwithstanding variations such as those resulting from schools of different sizes, in different locations and with a different clientele, and, in a few instances, significant alternative approaches, these generalisations apply widely in both primary and secondary schools, as many of the submissions to this review and a good number of research studies testify. They provide recognisable foundations for contemporary practice and very largely determine the goals and strategies for change. A conspicuous illustration is the provision of special education for children with learning impairments and difficulties, and of guidance and counselling services. These are examples of practices which arise from a well defined need that can only be met by departing from or adding to the mainline of educational practice. In Ireland, as elsewhere, it has proved easier to introduce the relatively infrequent major innovations of this kind than to transform the foundations. Reform in school organisation and practice may be regarded, therefore, as a combination of adjustments and modifications -- some highly significant, such as the abolition of the end of primary school examination -- and the occasionally wholly new structure.

The primary-secondary divide

The historically different functions of primary and secondary education have produced discontinuities in pedagogical style and curriculum approaches, one of the most significant being the single, generalist teacher model in the primary school as distinct from the subject specialist in the secondary school. Thus, transition arrangements have been and remain a focus of concern. Other reform proposals, which have had varying degrees of success, have been addressed to: premature selection for further education at the end of both primary and secondary schooling but mainly the former; pupil stratification through early streaming; instruction-dominated pedagogy; the gulf between the organisation of life within schools and in the home, community and workplace; the way in which school life is generally affected by selection and examination requirements. All these concerns and others to do with school organisation and practice have been widely aired and extensively documented, whether in the research and policy literature or in reviews and reports, of which there have been many in the past decade, and are the subject of many of the submissions for this review, not least the Department's Background Report.

It is a mark of the durability of the long-established forms of school and classroom organisation and of pedagogical practice, however, that reform proposals, where introduced at all, have generally proceeded at a slow pace and in the face of a great deal of scepticism. School amalgamation has been a continuing issue, causing controversy, particularly in rural areas. Despite a programme of amalgamation extending over decades, almost half of the country's 3 300 primary schools have three or fewer teachers. Some schools seem too large and others too small, but in practically every instance amalgamation is a battle to be fought and increasing public/parental participation will ensure that such kinds of restructuring will often be slow and difficult. Small schools are discussed below.

The reorganisation of secondary education, proposed by Education Ministers in the 1960s, and followed through a number of settings, has had a chequered history. The several parties involved seem to accept the different types of secondary schools as a workable compromise, freeing energies for concentration on such major issues as curriculum reform and school-work transition.

The familiar contours of schooling

The face that the Irish school presents to the world is thus quite recognisably that of previous generations. There is a growing dissonance between it and the development of learning sciences and modern teaching technologies that requires a very different approach. The design of buildings and teaching spaces is very largely predicated on a home-room class teacher in primary schools and a mixture of home-rooms and subject areas in secondary schools. Since many buildings have outlived their usefulness and cannot be readily or economically adapted, or are located in areas of declining school age population, the scope for improvement is considerable given that the necessary resources can be made available.

Co-operative (team) teaching and non-instructional forms of learning have not been conspicuous elements in determining school design and layout in the past, although in recent years many buildings have been made much more attractive, functional and flexible. Collections of separate classrooms with attendant facilities for laboratory work, physical education, craftwork and routine instruction in the schools for older children correlate with the structuring of the curriculum through discrete subjects and timetabled lessons of more or less fixed length. The mode of reporting on pupil performance through competitive assessments of the "visible" products of learning; the structuring of lessons around texts or other predefined units of learning such as formal tasks and assignments; the formal authority-based relationships between teachers and taught are also natural correlates of the basic design and layout of schools: each draws upon and reinforces the other. Large classes are accommodated simply by putting more desks, tables and chairs into existing rooms or adding portable classrooms where permanent buildings are not erected. Owing to the stratified nature of secondary education, and in response to a tradition of separate schools for boys and girls, in many small towns and suburbs there may be three or four smallish second level schools each physically similar to the others and organised in much the same way but serving different clienteles. None is comprehensively equipped or resourced and the opportunities for sharing are limited by physical and organisational considerations as much as by the traditional attitude that each school is its own, self-sufficient domain of learning. Relations with feeder primary schools vary but, given their physical separateness, the different patterns of school organisation to be found in them, and the different educational and training backgrounds of most secondary and primary teachers, these relations are often quite distant. As noted, primary to second-level transition is therefore a significant issue and many of the submissions and proposals we received referred directly to the necessity for a concerted attack on this problem.

The problematic nature of change and development

It is evident that, after a long period when education for the majority of the population was clearly inadequate in form and grossly under-resourced, there has been great progress since the 1960s in both the curriculum and the practice of schooling. Yet, despite the many changes in the direction of less formalism in relations -- more diversity of materials and a wider repertoire of teaching procedures, including self-directed and small group work -- and in the actual content of what is taught (for example in history, environmental studies, mathematics), the structural features and the organisation of schools and classrooms have proved very stable in Irish society. The greatest change has occurred, and is occurring, in secondary schools. Stability of form is not exclusive to Ireland; it is noteworthy across many if not all education systems. It must cause all educators to think carefully about the reasons for the persistence of key organisational features and to ponder for some time before embarking upon reforms that may prove to be misguided or ephemeral.

Yet there is undoubtedly a mismatch between the stated goals of education and the declared needs for substantial structural change in the society, on the one hand, and substantial areas of school practice, on the other. Several of these policy and goal statements refer directly to changes in school organisation. There have been many struggles over attempts to achieve reform, not only in the reorganisation of secondary education along comprehensive lines to which we have already referred.

Public expectations and assumptions about schooling are frequently tacit rather than explicitly stated. There seems to be general satisfaction, at any rate with the efforts schools make to educate younger children. This is not to say that public dialogue on educational issues is in any way lacking. So far as there is dissatisfaction with secondary education, it arises as much from the continuing high levels of unemployment as from the performance of the schools. The public appears to support stability as much as change. Thus, it would be wrong to jump hastily to the frequently drawn conclusions that, because reform is needed, "the school" lags sadly behind "the society" and that schooling belongs to the old-fashioned sector of modern society. Critics of schooling appear to be in a minority, although their challenges and expectations derive, for the most part, from a range of economic and social values in whose advancement they wish the school to be actively enlisted. Increasingly, however, this minority has been more visible and vocal and there is no question that broader governmental and societal objectives for the Ireland of the future will require for their achievement substantial developments in the very nature and quality of schooling. Inter-relationships between the overall provision and organisation of schools, curriculum, pedagogy and internal school organisation, on the one hand, and the socio-economic context, on the other, are undoubtedly complex and subtle regardless of the size of the country.

Small schools

Within recent years many OECD countries have been facing the problem of what to do about their small schools. On grounds of economy of scale, should they not be shut down and replaced by amalgamated schools of viable size? On organisational and curricular grounds, is it not desirable that all primary schools should have at least six classrooms and one all-purpose bigger room? At the secondary level, is it not essential to create large schools in order to deliver a broadly based curriculum and offer a wide range of facilities? For a time, it appeared that the advocates of economic rationalisation were winning the argument. More recently, it has become clear that most national authorities are favouring the retention of small primary schools on social and environmental as well as educational grounds, and maintaining many secondary schools at the minimum size required to deliver a balanced curriculum.

The authors of the report *Investment in Education*, aligning themselves with the economic rationalists, had much to say about the high cost of maintaining small schools[2], especially in view of what they demonstrated to be their inferior academic results *vis-à-vis* large schools[3]. From the early 1960s an active policy was adopted of closing small schools wherever possible. However, Ireland, despite its limited geographical area, still has a large number of small primary schools with only one to three teachers. Take the case of Protestant primary schools. "Twenty-three per cent of the number have only one teacher. Two-teacher schools account for a further thirty eight per cent. Altogether, over seventy-five per cent of the Protestant national schools have three or fewer teachers and only about two per cent of the total have non-teacher principals"[4]. This means, of course, that many primary school teachers face the challenge of dealing with two or several different age groups. At the secondary level, schools are also small by international standards, except for some of the newer community and comprehensive schools: 145 or 28 per cent of secondary schools have fewer than 300 pupils; only 22 have more than 800 pupils; 135 out of 246 vocational schools have fewer than 300 pupils, that is, more than half.

It is to be noted that at least two OECD countries, Norway and Germany, whose secondary systems are generally considered to function effectively, believe in the virtues of small secondary schools. In Germany, most schools have 400 pupils and a good number have fewer. Only the largest *Gymnasia* go up to around 800. As in Ireland, it is the few comprehensive schools that have over 1 000 pupils. The arguments used to sustain the case for smaller schools are that they provide an intimate ethos conducive to learning and that they enable the staff to give more personal attention to each pupil.

So it may be concluded that Ireland, which has conserved small schools for circumstantial reasons, is now in step with the international trend. It should strive, however, to encourage amalgamations aiming at four-teacher primary schools and secondary schools with as near to 400 pupils as the distribution of the local population will allow. At the same time, it should also try harder to arrange for small schools, especially at the secondary level, to share staff, space, laboratories, libraries and learning aids. Above we recommended the creation of local coordinating agencies. The examiners would also recommend that careful consideration should be given to developing distance learning techniques.

School-family-community: A tissue of relationships

In Chapter 2 we stressed that, according to the Irish Constitution, "the primary and natural educator of the child is the family". That statement would seem to imply that parents play a major role in Irish education. The reality is otherwise. They certainly have the right to choose the school to which to send their children -- even if many parents cannot exercise the right because of their family circumstances -- but so far they have exerted little pressure on schools either as a collective group or as individuals. In the main, parents have left the business of education to the schools, believing that the schools know best. For their part, managers, principals and teachers have scarcely encouraged the intervention of parents. This has not precluded good, informal relations between schools and parents being maintained, notably at the primary level, or the arrangement at many schools of regular parent-teacher meetings.

It was only as recently as 1985, however, that a National Parents' Council was established, that people began to speak of the need for local parents' associations as well, and that, in general, the idea began to be entertained that parents should be actually, and not merely constitutionally, partners in the educational process.

It was not until the early 1970s that parents became eligible for election to the Boards of Management of primary schools. The emergence of parent power, the presence of parents on management boards, and the proliferation of parents' associations have evident implications for the way schools and teachers conduct their relations with parents, and for the pre-service and in-service training of teachers.

School and home-family relationships are of special importance at the primary stage. Here the increasing activities of parent bodies pose a challenge to teachers brought up on the old understanding that the school gate was an effective barrier to parental involvement in school affairs. The pattern of organisation of primary education is broadly unitary -- the national school embodies entrenched beliefs and values concerning family-school-Church and, increasingly, State relations. This is a situation in which different partners, at different times and in different ways, take the lead. The Church and the teaching profession have been dominant; now they are increasingly sharing their authority with the parents. This is not merely a matter of parent power. After all, the child's home and family background has long had a significant impact upon the organisation of school and classroom -- hence the "home"-room, the single class teacher as parent surrogate and the attention given to interpersonal relations and a home-like atmosphere in the classroom. We have been struck by the number of references to the shifting balance in the school-home authority relationship, when the emphasis is clearly and consistently on the need for the school and the teacher to adapt still further to enable parents and parent organisations both locally and nationally to share the decisions about how schooling is organised and conducted.

Secondary education is organisationally diverse, or fractured, according to the observer's point of view. Here the participation of the family is far less direct and more diffuse. The most obvious extra-school influence is over the direction towards which each student is headed rather than that from which he or she has come. Hence, the increasing emphasis on patterns of school organisation which encourage work experience and out-of-school learnings. It is likely that this influence will increase markedly, as the more utilitarian orientation of second level gathers momentum. Teachers will themselves require a deeper knowledge of and insight into the requirements of the workplace than has normally been the case. Commercial and industrial and other employer groups will play a greater role not only in commenting on the performance and the potential of the young employee but also on how schools are run, and determining quality criteria and measures for improvement. The organisation and practice of secondary education will thereby become both more visible and more directly accountable to outside agencies. Teacher roles and responsibilities are affected by this trend as a wider responsibility for linking the practice of education with the realities of family and working life is added to their instructional and custodial functions.

Whatever the socio-economic expectations and needs may be, education remains constitutionally a parental and not an employer responsibility. When, despite vicissitudes, the family remains vital to individual well-being and when parents are increasingly conscious of themselves as a corporate body with common interests and the potential for real influence, it is necessary to underline the need for teachers to show a greater openness towards parental involvement than has been common in the past. Teachers must also develop a wider repertoire of skills and practices for relating to parents and involving them in school affairs. Parents, of course, wish to see education develop in a concrete and positive way the aptitudes and qualities of the individual child -- their child. They will weigh in the balance the more global and often utopian-sounding goals of society-wide change and nationally-defined requirements.

It is fruitful to see school organisation and practice in Ireland within a three-way relationship: *i)* the traditions, values and implicit assumptions of a well established and still generally well regarded social institution, the school; *ii)* the beliefs and expectations of the parents which, on the whole, seem to reinforce rather than to challenge the more traditional approaches to schooling; *iii)* the insistent demands at the level of the whole society for modernisation and a range of far-reaching structural changes which, to be effective, must incorporate changes in schooling.

Expressed in this way, the problems of school reform and teacher education may seem much more apparent than the answers. From the evidence we have examined, it cannot be concluded that there is any one dominant or powerful train of thought. Yet there is a gathering sense, as much among the teachers' organisations, the public education authorities and the higher education institutions as among outside critics and commentators, of the urgency of bringing seriously into question the pattern of school organisation and the widespread forms of practice within the school.

Reform: Piecemeal or root and branch?

The reform of schooling in the circumstances we have outlined seems to many to be more likely to result from the steady introduction of specific and usually limited innovations that, little by little, bring about a transformation, than by any dramatic interventionist policy. Others are impressed by the reserve power of the minister and what could be achieved through the stronger, more comprehensive and better articulated central planning and co-ordinating apparatus advocated in Chapter 3. The question is not just whether piecemeal and slow adjustments make sense in light of the wider changes and adaptations the country as a whole seems to be seeking, but whether the means exist, or could be created, to give to school organisation and pedagogical practice a new lease of life. To put it bluntly, the "steady as she goes" approach may as easily result in a downward as in an upward spiral. It cannot be assumed that modest, piecemeal change will bring about an improved quality and relevance of schooling. On the contrary, it could have the reverse effect. But no less salutary is the realisation that the apparatus for comprehensive change and development, where it exists at all, is on a modest scale.

A key question in shaping future policy for schooling is whether or not the present divisions are to be retained, strengthened or overcome. While there is widespread consensus about the undesirability of the present sharp break between primary and secondary schooling, there is no such agreement in respect of the divided pattern of secondary schools. Policy initiatives might, therefore, be best directed towards improving relations and arrangements among the different kinds of schools, for example in sharing resources, including teaching staff, joint programme planning and facilitating the transfer of students from one school to another. For this purpose, amalgamations are not required but formal affiliation could be beneficial, leading over time to a measure of programme integration and joint planning.

In considering ways of adapting, adjusting and further developing the organisation and practice of schooling the question arises: who are the agents and agencies for change? We shall discuss the role of teacher education and teacher educators, which must be seen in this light, in Chapter 7. A major potential resource at central level exists in the form of the inspectorate, which freed, as we have suggested, from some of its present tasks could make an invaluable contribution to curriculum and other development projects and provide informed assistance and advice in addressing organisational and pedagogical problems at the school level.

For systematic intervention to work in a large, expensive sector where there are thousands of highly educated, socially active and articulate individual agents -- the teachers and their associations -- strenuous efforts are required to generate sound strategies and seek consensus about both the need and the directions for change in the most intimate areas of professional life -- the organisation of the school and the practice of pedagogy.

But we are not aware that such efforts are being made or even thought to be necessary. It is not surprising, therefore, that there is no obvious body or agency to generate discussion and to advise the minister on policy. Elsewhere in this report, we suggest that it would be desirable to establish just such a body or to strengthen and enlarge the scope of existing agencies.

Any minister or government has to be convinced that there are powerful reasons for seeking fundamental changes in the ways schools are organised and teaching is carried out, if they are to justify the introduction of new machinery. More to the point, no new machinery ought to be installed until the potential of what already exists has been exhaustively explored and unless it can be shown that other strategies, for example increased in-service opportunities for teachers or new training programmes for principals, would not do as well. The argument we wish to propound is that, assuming the Department to be the principal instrument of intervention, it is necessary to identify strategic needs and to indicate how they can best be addressed in the closest possible collaboration with schools, teachers and communities.

Suggested directions

As the first stage in this endeavour, it is obviously essential to specify the principal changes in school organisation and practice that are most likely to produce a positive improvement in educational quality and the relevance of practice to wider societal concerns. What are these changes? The full answer to that question is that further dialogue and debate are required within Ireland. On the interim evidence before them, the examiners would recommend the following directions:

1. Data on the performance and quality of educational practice at the school level are not as comprehensive as they could be and such collections and analyses as are made are either not published at all or are issued years after the event. Monitoring of the school, reviews of its achievements, limitations and needs and the pinpointing of aspects of practice that require attention, would all benefit substantially from having a unit responsible for statistical data gathering and analysis within or closely associated with the Department of Education.

2. Within the policy framework, basic education should be affirmed in organisational terms as continuity throughout the whole period of compulsory schooling.

3. Increased flexibility and variety in the organisation of teaching and learning are needed in order to break down many of the present rigidities affecting the timetable, length of lessons, homework and so forth. The single, homogeneous class and the instructional models associated with it are not conducive to co-operative team work or to innovative approaches to teaching and learning.

4. The constraints, among which by universal consent lack of resources is the most pressing, should be systematically identified through monitoring, evaluation and research.

5. Any reduction in the pupil/teacher ratio at both the primary and secondary level should be conditional on negotiated agreements with teachers'

representatives to carry out such reforms as those outlined in the succession of reports since the time of the introduction of the new primary school curriculum.

6. Parental involvement in school decision-making has recently developed but is still at a fairly rudimentary stage. It is desirable to take much further the definition of, and support for, parental roles in school governance and decision-making. This is both a policy issue and a matter of detailed planning. Parent bodies seem willing to participate.

7. The training of principals and others in positions of senior responsibility, as managers of school organisations which are complex and outward-looking, is essential so that modern management, for example in planning, decision-making, resource management, accountability, interpersonal and community relations, can become more widespread in schools. It is important to develop a stratum of middle management in the larger schools.

8. The training and retraining of teachers should emphasize their role as articulators, managers and organisers of learning and not purveyors of facts and coaches for examinations, in order to enable them to cope positively with parent and community involvement in schooling and to acquire more democratic and co-operative values.

9. The organisation of the school day and of individual lessons should provide greater scope for more creative and imaginative problem-solving, skills enhancement, and practice-oriented approaches to learning. Students, as they mature, should be shouldering more responsibility for their own learning and at every stage they should be encouraged to display more initiative and independence of mind.

10. Streaming, setting and assessment by competitive examinations should be modified since, while facilitating a high standard of learning and excellent achievement by the minority, they scarcely benefit the majority of students.

11. More broadly, the organisation and practice of schooling should give greater scope for teachers as well as students to develop and apply a wide repertoire of skills in thinking, problem-solving, creative activity and social interaction.

NOTES AND REFERENCES

1. The examiners have been informed that the primary school sector is currently under internal review. They hope that their comments on that sector, in this and the following chapter, will serve as a contribution to that review.
2. "The general conclusion which emerges from the various indicators of benefits (number of post-primary scholarships, age/standard progression of pupils, curriculum available, and school facilities) is that the small schools do not appear to provide any greater educational benefits for their pupils which would offset their greater costs. The inference, indeed, is in the opposite direction, namely, that the smaller schools confer lesser benefits on their pupils" (*Cf. Investment in Education,* p. 252).
3. "Hence it may be concluded that in terms of teaching resources used, smaller schools cost per pupil anything from one-third to one-half more than larger schools" (*Ibid.,* p. 270).
4. *Submissions,* p. 15.

Chapter 5

THE SCHOOLS, VALUES AND THE CURRICULUM

Curriculum directions

In Chapter 3 we argued for a considerable strengthening of the central policy-making apparatus in combination with a devolution of responsibility for management and delivery of educational programmes. In this chapter we wish to draw attention to the importance, in any such development, of clarity and concreteness in the definition of the broad goals for schooling. Goals should embrace values, curriculum, pedagogy and school organisation. They should identify key actors and strategies and provide a lead for concerted action that requires a more co-ordinated and stronger initiative at the national level. Such an initiative does not preclude local and school-based effort; far from it, since without them any national strategy is doomed to failure.

Numerous attempts have been made during the 1970s and 1980s to plan for and implement a variety of curriculum reforms in primary and secondary schools. The most striking initiative was undoubtedly the new primary school curriculum introduced in 1971, following the abolition of the primary school certificate in 1967. In the spirit of the international reform movement in the 1960s and in the light of research findings, the underlying thrust of *Curaclam Na Bunscoile* (Primary School Curriculum) was to give learning and teaching much more of a child orientation, to foster such qualities as creativity, self-reliance, initiative and co-operation among children and to open up and broaden the range of studies well beyond the traditional pattern of basic learning. As in many other countries, the aspirations and language of the reformers outstripped the readiness and willingness of the system as a whole to respond. There was a shortfall which to this day is keenly felt. The reasons given vary from the inadequacy of planning, implementation, follow-through and resources, to teacher conservatism.

There is no doubt, however that the very production of this important document marked a new direction for educational thought and practice in Ireland. It remains to this day a key source of reference for new thinking about the curriculum for primary-age children. The more recent work of the National Council for Curriculum and Assessment has carried forward this momentum, although in the educationally more cautious era of the mid-1980s. The general orientation now gives greater emphasis to a firm, subject-oriented structure for the curriculum and to quantifiable student performance than was the case in the late 1960s and early 1970s.

For secondary curriculum reform there has been no document corresponding to the 1971 *Curaclam* for primary schools. Here the main determinants have been, and remain, the examination system with its bias towards further and higher education and the perceived requirements of working life. The general character of secondary curricula is drawn, on the one side, from the academic, subject-central tradition with a narrowing of the subject focus as specialisation takes over in the later years, and, on the other, from the vocational tradition with its emphasis on practical and manual skills. Beyond these two main thrusts, the secondary curriculum reveals a gender imbalance, with a concentration of boys in the scientific, technical and trade subjects and of girls in the humanities and secretarial, clerical and domestic subjects. There has been a considerable expansion of offerings in recent years, mainly in the practical/technically-based subjects, including commercial subjects and computing. Changes have occurred in other areas as a result of curriculum development projects and in recognition of the need for a wider repertoire of performance skills. The gender imbalance in the curriculum has also been modified but much more slowly than seems desirable to its critics.

The curriculum criticised

Notwithstanding the numerous and varied critiques, proposals, development projects and local initiatives, it seems that in neither primary nor secondary schools has a satisfactory curriculum balance been struck. There is dissatisfaction with present practice and frustration that new initiatives are being ignored or pursued with insufficient vigour. This ranges from disappointment by the Department and others at the limited impact of the 1971 *Curaclam*, through the view of the Joint Managerial Body for Secondary Schools that there are too many barriers and inhibitions in the management system, to the pressure from employer groups and tertiary bodies for more emphasis on scientific, technical and practical work in schools[1]. The establishment of the National Council for Curriculum and Assessment is the most important innovation in recent years, since it can provide the means whereby a national approach to the curriculum at both primary and secondary levels can be adopted, and the roles of the schools in implementing national guidelines and in developing their own approaches can be elaborated. There is much to be done in this regard, seeing that the necessary infrastructure for system-wide curriculum development has to be systematically built up, a task requiring both better co-ordination of existing agencies and the installation of new structures.

There was widespread agreement among those interviewed by the examiners that the curriculum has become too static in its original instrumental and academic orientations and that the process of change by accretion has, in Ireland as elsewhere, produced overload without the requisite reorganisation. In its 1985 *Discussion Paper on Primary Education*, the Curriculum and Examinations Board recognised this problem and proposed a broad "areas-of-experience" approach. Necessary as it is to maintain the highest levels of academic performance in primary as well as in secondary schools, it is of no less importance to ensure that a modern, stimulating curriculum for all children be put in place.

Despite the vision and thoroughness of the 1971 primary schools curriculum proposals and the many practical innovations since carried through by dedicated teachers, the evidence suggests that emphasis is still largely on a didactic approach and often, in later primary years, in a relatively narrow range of subject matters. The latter reflects the continuing dominance over some parts of the system of selective secondary schools and the examinations for which they prepare so effectively, while the former is a result of a long pedagogical tradition which teachers need a great deal of support and encouragement to enlarge and broaden. The implications for teacher training will be discussed in Chapter 7.

The domination of examinations, particularly at the upper secondary level, ensures that, on the one hand, teaching and the curriculum are largely determined by examination requirements, and, on the other, that major status differences persist throughout the secondary system, between the examination streams and the rest. These problems were acknowledged in a number of the submissions received and in the examiners' discussions with a wide variety of educational organisations and representatives. They feature in the 1986 report of the Curriculum and Examinations Board, *In Our Schools*, and in the follow-up consultative document, *Senior Cycle Development and Direction*.

Reference to the curriculum section of the Department's *Rules and Programme for Secondary Schools 1987-88* provides a clue: teachers and the educational community generally are confronted by a bald list of required and approved subjects with their syllabuses and examinations requirements, and it is to this that they are responding. The introduction of a new examination at the end of the lower secondary stage provides opportunities for a wider appraisal of the curriculum. That this is required is indicated by the fact that nowadays in excess of 90 per cent of young people remain in full-time education until the end of the lower secondary cycle whereas, as recently as twenty years ago, only two-thirds of those leaving primary school proceeded to any form of post-primary education, and of those going on, more than a third left without sitting for any public examination. The lower secondary school has become a universal and not simply a mass institution, and its curriculum ought to be revised accordingly. Consequently, *In Our Schools* outlined an integrated "areas of experience" approach with a core drawn from: arts education; guidance and counselling; language and literature; mathematical studies; physical education; religious education; science and technology; social, political and environmental studies. For each area, elements of learning (knowledge, concepts, skills and attitudes) were to be determined. The Board, however, conceded a great deal to subject-centred teaching by claiming that existing subjects should be the "starting point", and this is reflected in the current policy of a subject-based curriculum culminating in the new Junior Certificate.

At the primary level, notwithstanding the significant gains since 1971, the curriculum still reveals, to a greater extent than many Irish educators wish to see continued, a great deal of the character of a watered-down and extended form of the old elementary education with its emphasis on predefined and narrow performance standards in the traditional basics, together with religious, moral and civic instruction. Such milestones as the abolition of the Primary Certificate examination in 1967, the extension of pre-service training for future primary teachers from two to three years with much greater emphasis on modern pedagogy, and the establishment of the primary school as the first major phase of a process of continuing education for everyone, together with the 1971 report, set a new direction. However, pedagogical practice at this stage is still often modelled on that of the individual teacher in charge of a single class with relatively little co-operative team teaching and too little scope for activity learning. As long as financial constraints inhibit the education authorities from providing adequate resources and equipment and making significant reductions in the pupil/teacher ratio, these features are likely to endure. Consequently, as the main primary teachers' union, INTO, has stated, there is an excessive reliance on textbooks for source materials and less stretching of pupils' horizons than is desirable[2].

At the secondary level, as the Background Report affirms, the curriculum is a derivation from the "classical humanist" tradition with an overlay of technological/technical/vocational subjects and a leavening provided by development projects. The increasing diversity of the student population, consequent upon increased retention rates, presents a challenge to curriculum planners and, indeed, substantial changes have been foreshadowed in the consultative document prepared by the National Council for Curriculum and Assessment.

Broadly speaking, the Irish school curriculum is split in a way that corresponds with the divided school system -- both vertically (primary-secondary) and horizontally within the secondary level. Even now curriculum planning treats primary and secondary levels as quite distinctive and separate, and therefore transition problems are an inevitable consequence. At the secondary level, the elements of the classical humanist tradition are embedded in the curriculum of the secondary schools and to some extent in that of the comprehensive and community schools, in a set of academic subjects leading to the leaving certificate, and for those who succeed in crossing this hurdle, to professional and executive careers. By contrast, the curriculum of the vocational and technical schools is more practical and more overtly related to occupations and careers in manual, trades, clerical and secretarial fields and middle-management positions. In practice, this polarisation is often less extreme than here presented, since secondary schools do provide for less academic pupils to a greater or lesser degree and the vocational and technical schools do try to give access for some to higher-level technological and scientific education and the relevant career openings. Over and above that distinction, the comprehensive and community schools have shifted their curricula into the wide range of channels familiar in the comprehensive school movement internationally.

Towards instrumental and utilitarian values

As a result of the gathering interest in career-related and work-oriented secondary education, Ireland, in common with most other OECD countries, has sought throughout the 1980s to strengthen the more socially instrumental and utilitarian elements of its school and higher education curriculum. These changes are not, however, merely a further illustration of the gearing of schools to meet social demand. For the much more diverse student population in secondary education, they are likely to produce more relevant and motivating programmes of study. At the primary level, the renewed interest in defining the fundamental tools and skills of learning is likewise a response both to a social concern that education at all stages should be so organised as to prepare young people for effective social participation, and a concern that every young person needs to be able to cope with the learning tasks of secondary and, increasingly, post-secondary education. It is perhaps too soon to say how far this curriculum policy orientation is likely to succeed. In practice, as we have already indicated, there are constraints and barriers that will be difficult to surmount.

In secondary schools, the curriculum problem emerges in its most acute form. The weight of the classical humanist tradition is enormous, not least because of its underpinning of high-status occupations and a way of life which is widely admired even though unattainable by the majority. This dominance is likely to prevail unless the authorities are able to develop either a much more powerful parallel system of technical/vocational schools or a restructured general secondary education curriculum. For the early years of the secondary cycle, the dichotomy is less sharp. The technical/vocational thrust is being sustained at the same time as the new certificate to be awarded at the completion of secondary education is being introduced. It is at the upper secondary level that directions are much less clear.

Equality of opportunity and the needs of the under-achieving pupils

Equality of opportunity has been a major aim of Irish educational policy since the early 1960s. *Investment in Education* pointed out that there was "a very marked association between social group and participation in full time education" and that "it has been traditional in Ireland to separate children into different types of schools, especially at the post-primary level, on the basis of a number of criteria, such as sex, religion, linguistic orientation, social class, and educational orientation". The report added: "In view of the apparent seriousness of this phenomenon it would seem to merit full examination"[3]. It also stressed that besides inequality arising from socio-economic background there was an uneven distribution of educational opportunities across the country, especially at the secondary level.

To a satisfying degree geographical inequality at the secondary level has since been removed thanks to the provision of free transport, the creation of the new comprehensive and community schools, and the broadening of the curriculum as well as the intake of vocational schools. There can be satisfaction, too, in the extension of compulsory schooling by one year, the greatly increased retention rate at the post-compulsory level, and the wider range of education and training opportunities now open to 16-19 year-olds. The fact remains, however, that inequality persists. About 15 per cent of pupils are not achieving a satisfactory result at the end of compulsory schooling, and the great majority of them come from poor families living in deprived areas.

No one today questions that serving the needs of under-achieving pupils is a high educational priority. It is generally recognised, as in other countries, that, despite all the improvements of recent times, a disturbingly large percentage of pupils do not master even basic knowledge and skills. They fall behind at an early age and, as the years go by, their motivation crumbles and the learning gap between them and pupils of average ability inexorably widens. On arriving at the end of compulsory schooling they are not qualified for employment and unequipped with survival skills to fend adequately for themselves in adult life.

It is also generally recognised, again as in other countries, that the great majority of under-achieving pupils are located in economically disadvantaged neighbourhoods and that, in these neighbourhoods, some schools have more under-achieving pupils than others. General recognition of the under-achievement phenomenon has been complemented by the efforts of educationists and researchers to measure its extent, to analyse the reasons for it, to study the experiences of other countries in trying to cope with it, and to propose strategies for action. All appear to agree that the source of the problem is social and cultural at least as much as educational, and that close home/school links are indispensable[4]. Many believe that high pupil/teacher ratios present an insuperable barrier on the school side (see Chapter 6), not least at the pre-school level where classes tend to be large and where it is important to give children at risk an early exposure to learning. A few postulate a community-development approach to the problem. The over-riding implication of all the proposals is that more specialist staff are required.

The Programme for Action in Education 1984-87 recommended the strategy of appointing additional teachers to primary schools in disadvantaged areas. The Department of Education can approve the appointment of remedial teachers in addition to the regular staffing establishment. During the year 1986/87, there were 857 teachers in this category. Some were serving more than one school so that the total number of schools being assisted was 1 100. Priority is accorded to schools in economically disadvantaged neighbourhoods. The examiners heard two criticisms of the present arrangements. The first was that many more remedial teachers were required if the needs of all under-achieving pupils were to be met. That is unquestionably true but, given the current climate of stringent budgetary control, the scale of the commitment is still considerable. No doubt it should have a prior claim on any additional funds that become available. The practice of using remedial teachers to serve more than one school is criticised on the grounds that time is lost as they move from one site to another, and that timetabling becomes complicated. Against this, the practice makes for flexibility since some schools may require only minimal remedial services whereas others may require a great deal of assistance.

The examiners wish, in conclusion, to utter a word of warning. The United States experience of pulling pupils out of their regular classes under the Title I compensatory programme proved to be a mistake. A better strategy is to provide extra funds to schools with a large number of children at risk and to leave each school to identify, diagnose and find appropriate ways of serving individual needs.

Learning foreign languages

In Chapter 1 we stressed the importance attached by Ireland to the European connection in general and the value of the EEC in particular. In order to foster this connection, however, it is evident that the study of foreign languages and civilisations requires strong reinforcement. The incentive to learn modern languages is weak in all English-speaking countries because of the extraordinary dominance of the English language in international communications. The urgent desire of "continental Europeans" to master English has not been paralleled by the same desire to speak French or German or Spanish in the United Kingdom, the United States or in Ireland. Yet Ireland has not only the same incentive as the two other countries to ensure that, in all sectors of commerce and industry, the workforce can communicate in foreign languages, but also a critical need to attract an ever-increasing number of tourists from other than anglophone countries.

The examiners suggest that consideration should be given to undertaking an inquiry into the adequacy of the present provision for foreign language teaching with special reference to its implications for the curriculum at the primary as well as the secondary level and for the preparation and in-service training of teachers.

Assessing and examining

Like many other OECD countries, Ireland has a pattern of public examinations, used as an implicit accountability mechanism and sorting device originally designed for a school system in which the great majority of young people were expected to enter the labour market at the end of compulsory schooling, while only a minority proceeded to secondary education with a view to preparing for university entrance. The secondary syllabus was accordingly drawn up with university entrance in mind. This had the incidental effect of ensuring a very high degree of uniformity in the syllabuses offered from one secondary school to another.

Over time the syllabus has been greatly modified. The fact remains that, according to many educators and educationists, university entrance requirements continue to dominate the upper secondary school curriculum which, in turn, dominates the curriculum of the lower secondary level. Some critics argue further that teaching in the second stage of the primary school is often geared to the needs of the academically-motivated pupils whose parents already have their eyes set on the goal of university entrance, even though it is six to eight years distant. This is an articulation of stage levels of the wrong kind. Typical of the concern about the stranglehold on the curriculum of public examinations is the question posed in the submission of University College Dublin: "Can more be done to ensure that public exams become the servants rather than the masters of curriculum change?"[5].

It is widely agreed in Ireland that a major reform of assessment, examining and credentialling is long overdue[6]. Testing provides a mechanism by which to shape the instruction methods used in schools. Tests that emphasize skills and fragmented knowledge retrieval reward one kind of teaching. Tests that challenge students to explore new data and to form and defend theses will reward a very different kind of teaching. Reform should certainly be directed at the examination system if curriculum reform strategies are to succeed. This has happened already in primary schools and is under way for the junior secondary cycle. It remains to be addressed in the upper secondary schools. Whereas in its report *In Our Schools*, the Curriculum and Examinations Board outlined directions and a strategy for improvements in junior cycle assessing and examining, including a new certificate and increased roles for teachers in school-based assessments, it was almost completely silent on senior cycle examinations. The Board returned to the subject in its consultative document, *Senior Cycle: Development and Direction*, recommending a broader framework for the

Leaving Certificate, provision for school-based assessment and other modifications to cater for the diverse student population. A great deal more effort would be required to incorporate even these indicative changes into new national procedures for senior cycle assessment and examination.

It is often said that the reform of assessment and examinations should follow rather than precede curriculum reform. The reality is that teachers tend to teach to an examination, and administrators are inclined to seek simple, cost-effective ways of assessing students. Examining and assessing can play a crucial part in guiding curricular change. Thus, it is appropriate to discuss together both curriculum and assessing/examining, as the National Council for Curriculum and Assessment has been doing[7].

Among the improvements in assessment which are already occurring, the following could be more widely fostered as a way of meeting the needs of the whole student population instead of the minority: negotiated learning agreements, especially for older secondary school pupils; use of practical tasks and oral work in addition to written assignments and tests; incorporation of work experience, field work, projects and other out-of-school activities in the formal assessment process; graded tests and pupil profiles. In all these activities, teachers should be directly enlisted, as is appropriate for a responsible profession. Since, however, this would entail the acquisition of procedural and technical skills that are not, at present, widespread, provision for appropriate teacher in-service and pre-service programmes would be an essential prerequisite.

There is valuable international experience to draw upon in support of local endeavours in all of these assessment procedures, which could be channelled through the National Council for Curriculum and Assessment. That Council appears to be the organisation best fitted to continue wide-ranging reviews and further development of assessment and examination practices at both primary and secondary schooling, with a view to achieving a close match between curriculum, pedagogy and assessment practice. Changes in assessment and examining are inevitable, given the forces at work in Irish society and education. The policies and practices appropriate to minority participation in secondary schooling will no longer suffice in a universal system. The attempts being made to develop a broad, common core curriculum will certainly require novel arrangements for assessment and examinations.

The planning and design of a common core curriculum for all students throughout the whole period of compulsory schooling, embracing foundations for and the elements of the areas of experience outlined in the 1986 report *In Our Schools*, will necessarily incorporate a much wider repertoire of assessment practices. *In Our Schools* rightly, in our view, argued for a well planned continuity of experience between primary and secondary schooling, for the examinations to serve rather than manipulate the curriculum and for core areas of experience appropriately organised to meet varying student needs and aptitudes. A general strategy would integrate, not separate, designs for curriculum, teaching and learning processes, assessment and examinations. Implementation and follow-through have been, by general consent, given too little attention in the proposals emanating from the several reviews and inquiries of the past. We have indicated that these matters can now be addressed through the work of the National Council for Curriculum and Assessment and with the active support and involvement of an enlarged inspectorate having more concentrated functions.

While a core curriculum based on areas of experience and complemented by a range of optional and specialist studies should be the basis, it is equally necessary to emphasize the need for a range of pupil attainment targets rather than a unitary set which, in practice, favours the more academically gifted and socially privileged students. Both the broad curriculum framework and the set of pupil attainment targets ought to be national in character, but at such a level of generality as to serve as guidelines rather than prescriptive requirements. Thus, individual schools, operating as units, and engaging parents and community representatives as well as teachers, should be in a position to define curriculum details and precise attainment targets relevant to their own student populations and local requirements. The present system does not prevent this. On the contrary, such endeavours as the inspectorate's team-based *Plean scoile* (school plans) for the primary sector are a positive encouragement. But it is extremely difficult for schools to act in such a constructive way when resources are limited, class sizes are large, and the highest status is attached to the academic domain.

The rationale for continuing change in curriculum, assessment and examining

The suggestions put forward so far in this chapter entail a major reform of the education system extending over many years together with increased demands on resources. The question naturally arises whether change on this scale is necessary. Our first and most fundamental response is that we have made no suggestions that have not already been proposed and discussed by Irish educators themselves and that do not form the staple of official reports and documents. The major source of these ideas is the succession of reports and proposals following the 1980 *White Paper on Educational Development* (the first ever Irish educational White Paper), although their antecedents lie in the endeavours in the 1960s to devise a comprehensive system of secondary education and to reshape primary education.

Notwithstanding differences in the topics addressed and stances adopted, there is an overall similarity of approach and homogeneity of conclusions in the substantial body of research and normative literature in Ireland. Perhaps the most pervasive concern is the need to modernise the school system by relating it in more direct ways to the cultural/socio-economic condition of the country in the present day and age, bearing in mind Ireland's interdependence within the international order. Thus, the definition of curriculum must incorporate social, cultural and economic data and involve participants beyond the field of education itself.

This social orientation is not separate from, but intimately related to, a concern that the values of the school, curriculum and pedagogy should be more responsive to individual student requirements. Time and again we were reminded that it is social change which is producing a generation of students for whom traditional forms of education are quite unsuited. Thus, recommendations concerning pedagogy focus on the need for the transformation of classrooms from traditional centres of instruction to active centres of learning where initiative, independence of thought, practical skills, problem-solving and cognitive strategies become central rather than marginal as they often are at present.

Our recommendations in support of a sequential common core curriculum throughout the years of compulsory schooling and of attendant changes in assessment and examination practice raise difficulties, to be sure, but they are not insuperable. On the technical side, the actual construction of a core curriculum which is common to students of widely different backgrounds, attainments, aptitudes and interests in learning presents problems to curriculum designers. No curriculum design which is centrally prescriptive in detail and precludes local adaptation is likely to succeed. Likewise, no design which avoids the task of structuring and adapting the content of the common learnings to the different intellectual capabilities of students will have a positive effect. Moreover, Irish education has demonstrated great strength both in its academic orientation, on the one hand, and in its provision of vocational opportunities on the other. This strength must not be lost.

One of the missing or under-developed links in the curriculum planning and decision-making system is the participation of the social partners, by which we mean representatives of the employment sector and of parents and community groups. The participation by parents as of right in school boards is a move in this direction; there is also a long tradition of employer involvement in vocational education. Thus, there is a foundation for the full involvement of the social partners in what is traditionally the well guarded professional preserve of curriculum and assessment. But the changes which Irish society is now contemplating with regard to the overall education system require more wide-ranging and systematic means of involving representatives of these sectors. Apart from the necessity of relating the content of changing curricula and the procedures for assessment to changing social realities, the agreement of such groups would be required. Their participation would also be a means whereby the current preoccupation with book and verbal knowledge accompanied by instructional modes of teaching and regurgitative practices in assessment and examinations could be reduced. It is also from such participation that there could be a greater recognition of the educational value for everyone of the industrial arts, the habits and practices of commerce, craftwork in wood and metal (of which we saw excellent examples) and other forms of manual and technical activity. Finally, with this wider social orientation, due attention could be given to such cross-curriculum themes as health education, environmental education, social and political education and others which, in the normal course of events, have to fight hard for recognition in schools.

To sum up: the basic goals and values of the education system have tended to be tacit rather than explicit during a period when major transformations in the society, economy and culture have been occurring; curriculum, assessment and examination changes have been continual but piecemeal. The need to make them explicit and to reconstruct them in the light of contemporary realities is now widely acknowledged, as is the need for a better resourced school system and a more comprehensive apparatus for planning and developing education. We have indicated our support for these changes, indicated some of the ways in which they may be carried through and pressed home some of their major implications for teacher education, both pre-service and in-service.

NOTES AND REFERENCES

1. "The consultants argue that the educational system has not responded sufficiently to current labour market requirements and may now require some modification. They cite, in particular, the over-emphasis on general education and the failure to develop a project higher cycle structure in the vocational sector" (*Cf. Manpower Policy in Ireland*, p. 6).
2. For a general discussion of improvements in the primary school curriculum since 1971 and pinpointing of continuing weaknesses cf. Irish National Teachers' Organisation, *Primary Curriculum and Related Matters: Report of a conference* (Dublin, 1988)
3. *Investment in Education*, p. 324 ff.
4. For example: "Access to, participation in and success derived from education were all found to be related to educationally irrelevant factors such as place of residence, gender (although this was not often adverted to and most significantly social background or socio-economic status" (Conference of Major Religious Superiors, Inequality in Schooling in Ireland (Dublin, 1988, p. ii). See also Irish National Teachers' Organisation, *Educational Disadvantage: Report of a seminar* (Dublin, 1984) *passim*.
5. *Submissions*, p. 108.
6. See, for example, Irish National Teachers' Organisation, *Assessment in the Primary School: discussion paper* (Dublin, 1986).
7. This was recommended in *The I.C.E. Report: Final Report of the Committee on the Form and Function of the Intermediate Certificate Examination*.

Chapter 6

WHAT TEACHERS?
IN WHAT NUMBERS? IN WHICH INSTITUTIONS?

What teachers?

The response given in Ireland to the query "what teachers" is likely to be an emphatic "teachers of high quality". Other countries may be lamenting a lack of good teachers and a concomitant decline in the overall status of the teaching profession, but not Ireland. The following extracts from two of the submissions to this review accurately reflect popular opinion:

"Education for the Irish has always been held in high esteem. It has traditional values in that, when the Irish had nothing else, they had the hedge school. The local teacher was a person of consequence in local society, acting as teacher but also as counsellor and peacemaker when necessary. These values still exist and it is true to say the teaching profession is one that is looked up to and is a popular choice of career for many school-leavers"[1].

"It can hardly be gainsaid that this country is fortunate in the quality of its teaching personnel"[2].

The evidence certainly endorses the thrust of that statement. Recruits to the colleges of education responsible for the training of primary school teachers have always been of particularly outstanding academic quality year after year. The colleges have received far more applications than there were places available, and all report that those selected for admission have obtained marks in their final school examination that would have comfortably guaranteed them a university place[3]. The overall quality of the intake to the university departments of education that prepare secondary school teachers has varied somewhat over time according to the number of places available, but is said to have been consistently good, although a teaching career has not been the first choice of many candidates. It is undoubtedly of high academic quality at the present time when the competition for places in most subjects is intense.

Most practising teachers have few reservations about their own professional competence and their good standing in society. Moreover, they enjoy certain satisfactory conditions of service. Their salaries are relatively high *vis-à-vis* other professions and compared with the low remuneration of teachers in certain other OECD countries[4]. Since 1969 there has been a common basic salary scale for all teachers regardless of the educational level that is taught. They have a short working year by the international reckoning. Their autonomy in the classroom is legendary. Their relations with their employing authorities are generally cordial. Finally, they belong to what will soon become an all-graduate profession.

The question at issue today, however, is whether the quality of the teaching force as a whole can be maintained over the years ahead against the changing social and cultural context described in preceding chapters and given that few young teachers will be appointed unless there is a major shift in supply policy. Despite the general level of satisfaction in the past, teachers have always lacked some of the typical characteristics of a profession. The close monitoring of primary schools by the inspectorate has sometimes inhibited and discouraged self-evaluation by individual teachers. The weak participation of teachers in curriculum development and action research has reduced their motivation to experiment and innovate. The absence of a substantial system of in-service training makes it difficult for them to keep their knowledge and skills up to date. Many are insufficiently equipped with the communications skills now required to engage in dialogue with parents, employers, and representatives of the community. The majority of teachers have had no prospect of rising to the post of principal or, indeed, to any post of responsibility.

In secondary schools, there is a specific constraint on true professionalism for a teacher may be required, at least in theory, to teach any subject in the curriculum. In practice, many do teach a subject (or subjects) which had not been their main strength when at university. By contrast, in vocational schools teachers must hold a formal qualification in the subject that they teach.

Notwithstanding, teachers have not been conscious until recently of any breach of their professional esteem. Now they are faced with unprecedented conditions that are likely to lead to soul-searching throughout the profession and to hard times in the classroom for some teachers. These conditions include:

  i)   uncertainty about future employment for young teachers;
  ii) the ineluctable ageing of the teaching force;
  iii) financial cut-backs that have led to higher pupil/teacher ratios and a reduction of supporting services;
  iv) fear of salaries declining in real money terms;
  v)   competition to keep posts alive while developing co-operation among schools;
  vi) more heterogeneous classes at the secondary level;

vii) the stress of having to adapt to a new curriculum;
viii) in some schools, emerging signs of indiscipline; in all schools more ebullient and challenging pupils.

On top of all these pressures, there is the prospect of teaching becoming an immobile profession as only a trickle of new entrants find their way into it. The great majority of practising teachers are under forty-five years of age (72 per cent in secondary education). Only relatively few will be retiring annually over the next decade or so. As a result, opportunities for career improvement and changes of post will dry up unless special incentives are created. As in other OECD countries, teaching will become a greying occupation. Will not professional knowledge and skills become rusty? Will not the traditional dedication of teachers become hard to sustain? Will not more and more teachers succumb to burn-out?

In Chapter 7 we intend to discuss possible ways and means of countering the new pressures to which teachers are exposed within the context of a new concept of the teaching career. Believing, however, that the emerging problems of the teaching force cannot be solved if there are to be very few new entrants, we propose to consider first the issue of teacher supply that lies at the heart of the matter.

What numbers?

The high birthrate, combined with rapidly increasing enrolments at the post-compulsory level from the early 1960s, ensured, along with other factors, including a fall in the pupil/teacher ratio (hereinafter PTR) and the appointment of more specialised teachers, that there was a steady increase in the demand for primary school teachers and a steep rise in the demand for secondary school teachers.

Since 1980, as we have seen, the birthrate has fallen and the annual increase in the retention rate at the post-compulsory level has flattened out. The available calculations of future trends show that there will be a pronounced decline at the primary level between 1989/90 and 2000/2001 of the order of 22 per cent, and a significant decline at the secondary level of the order of 11 per cent, mostly at the lower secondary level. At the same time, the government has enforced a policy of economic austerity. For education this has entailed a general squeeze on resources and a specific measure to raise the PTR to 27.6:1 in primary schools. The outcome of these several factors has been a sharp fall in the demand for additional teachers and the emergence of a critical rate of unemployment or under-employment among newly qualified teachers. The consequences for the training establishments have been traumatic and will be discussed below. Here, we propose to consider the ramifications of the supply and demand factor as they affect policy-making.

The assumption might be drawn that, subject to a small reduction in the PTR (see below PTR), there will be no change in the present level of demand for teachers for the foreseeable future. This would be unreasonable since both international[5] and national experience have demonstrated that long- and even medium- term forecasts of demand are difficult to make because there are so many unpredictable factors that are likely to invalidate them[6]. In Ireland, these could include an increase (or, indeed, further decline) in the fertility rate, a change in the emigration flows and a sudden increase in the retention rate at the post-compulsory level. At least, therefore, it would appear to be only prudent to allow some degree of flexibility in determining the total number of teachers that will be required in the future. Prudence is further called for by the fact that the mechanistic application of the PTR and specific coefficients make forecasts unlikely to be accurate.

But there are other important factors to be taken into account when seeking to anticipate the demand for teachers in the mid- and long-term future, apart from such factors as the broadening of the curriculum and the diversification of teachers' tasks:

   i)   the PTR;
   ii) the length of the secondary cycle;
   iii) the duration of the school year;
   iv) the incidence of teacher shortages in certain subjects and appointment of specialist teachers;
   v)   the strengthening of school management structures;
   vi) increased supervision of a prolonged period of induction and expansion of in-service training;
   vii) the export of teachers.

The pupil/teacher ratio

To judge from the documentary evidence and the pronouncements of interest groups, the issue of pupil/teacher ratios is, arguably, the most contentious in the whole field of education in Ireland. The device of the PTR is used to determine the number of staff to be allocated to each school both at the primary and secondary level. From the early 1960s there was a conscientious attempt to bring it down in primary schools by gradual stages as the following table illustrates:

Year	Enrolment	No. of teachers	Ratio
1961/62	484 618	14 091	34.4
1971/62	511 254	15 450	33.1
1981/62	556 434	19 926	27.9
1985/66	567 615	21 144	26.8

It is to be noted that, although enrolments increased by approximately 16 per cent, the PTR was reduced by as much as approximately 22 per cent. That was no mean achievement. However, owing to the recent budgetary cuts, the PTR has been allowed to rise to 27.6:1 on the understanding between the Government and the Irish National Teachers' Organisation that it will be steadily reduced so as to arrive at an expected 26.7:1 by 1990/91. The increase in the PTR has led to discontent. Some critics point out that, in practice, certain classes have 40 pupils, and that Ireland has the least favourable PTR among EEC countries for both primary and secondary education.

The high ratio is held culpable, among other factors, for the problem of dealing effectively with under-achievers, the inability of schools and teachers to innovate, increasing stress among teachers, the impossibility of assigning time during school hours for in-service training, and the inflexibility of the curriculum. The submission from the Froebel College of Education states: "Pupil/teacher ratio is one factor in the failure of full implementation of the *Primary* School Curriculum. An approach to teaching which allows direct child involvement in the learning process is very difficult in classes of thirty-five to forty children"[7]. It is also argued that there has been no real excess of teacher supply, the raising of the PTR having been used as a blunt instrument for reducing demand for teachers.

It is notoriously difficult to determine what is the ideal PTR and, in turn, class size[8]. There is certainly no exact correlation between the ratio and the performance of pupils. Thus, Japanese pupils come out best in international comparisons of academic attainment and yet the ratio in Japan is higher than in many other OECD countries. The overall international experience also reveals that lowering the ratio by one or more units has no measurable effect on cognitive outcomes. Of course, if it is argued that the ratio has no significance at all, treasury officials may well be pleased but teachers will rightly dismiss the argument as absurd. One rule of thumb is that a class is too big when the teacher can no longer give individual attention to each pupil.

Our purpose is to question the tendency to treat the blanket lowering of the PTR as the priority of priorities in terms of policy. Over the longer haul, a steady reduction will certainly be desirable as funds permit. In the meantime, any additional funds might be better expended on selective measures such as employing more teachers in disadvantaged schools (that is, a discriminatory lowering of the PTR), more teachers of specialist subjects at primary and secondary levels, introducing more instructional technology, and increasing the number of ancillary staff.

It is important to stress that we do perceive a need for more teaching and other staff but that we are wary of what appears to be an obsession in some quarters with lowering the overall PTR. On grounds of equity and teacher effectiveness we believe that a selective allocation of additional staff and targeted improvement are called for in order that the PTR can be used as a more finely-tuned policy option.

Duration of the secondary school cycle

At the present time, some secondary schools are funded so as to offer a complete six-year cycle (3 years lower; 3 years upper), whereas others are funded to offer a cycle of no more than five years (3 years lower; 2 years upper). This is an anomalous situation, all the more so in that the intake to the former schools might well be regarded as already more privileged in social class terms than the intake to the latter.

In any case, a five-year cycle of secondary schooling may be considered too short, not only because it is below the international average, but also because the demands of contemporary society call for a broadly-based and yet in-depth curriculum that cannot be contained within five years and adequately prepare for post-secondary studies or direct entry into working life. We further share the view of those in Ireland who consider that young people would benefit more from university-level studies if their age at entry was eighteen rather than seventeen or even sixteen.

To offer the possibility of completing a six-year cycle of schooling to all secondary students would necessarily entail the appointment of considerably more teachers. How many would depend on the speed with which the longer cycle is phased in and on the breadth of the sixth-year curriculum adopted. Planning estimates under a variety of options would be called for.

Length of the school year

In recent years research findings have multiplied to show that the amount of time that young people spend actually learning has a critical bearing on their academic and all-round performance. In all, the time dimension comprises the length of the school day, the length of the school year, the length of the complete schooling cycle, and the intensity of active learning (time on task)[9]. A recent report prepared by the United States Department of Education infers that the low attainment of American students in internationally-monitored tests is due, at least in part, to the much longer school year in other countries, notably in Japan[10].

In Ireland, some educationists have been expressing concern for many years about the length of the school year. Pupils attend school for five to six hours a day on five days a week for 184 days a year in primary schools and 180 days in secondary schools. This adds up to one of the lowest totals of annual hours among OECD countries. It might be claimed, of course, that "the time spent on task" is greater than elsewhere but that would be hard to prove. The shortness of the school year is compounded in secondary schools by the amount of time lost towards the end of the year by the inconveniences of administering the national examinations. Furthermore, it has to be noted that the timetable in Irish school calls for two and a half hours per week for religious studies and a varying number of hours a week for Irish language studies according to the level. Given the desire to continue to raise the educational level of the population, especially in view of the advent of the single European market from 1992, we would suggest that a review of the situation is urgently called for with a view to aligning the school year with that of most other countries.

It is evident that the teachers' associations would oppose any lengthening of the school year without some compensatory arrangements. By that we do not refer to an increase in salaries in exchange for more hours of work since teachers would argue that their present output of time and effort is already at the maximum that can be expected of them. Rather we would recommend that compensation should be in the form of some reduction in weekly contact hours and a regular allocation of time for professional development, mainly in the form of in-service training.

Lengthening the school year under the conditions we have described would entail the appointment of additional staff.

Appointment of specialised teachers

We sympathise with the view that specialist teachers should be appointed to the primary schools and that the psychological service at this level should be developed. There will also be a demand for more secondary teachers because of:

i) shortage subjects (sciences, foreign languages, business studies), which may coexist, as in many countries, with an overall surplus but unhappily there is no reliable data on this situation;

ii) a graduated increase of teaching posts following the adoption of a broader curriculum (arts and crafts, technology, foreign languages);

iii) greater recruitment of counsellors as well as remedial teachers in relation to the real needs of schools, specifically in socially deprived areas.

Strengthening school management structures

Under this rubric there are two factors that affect teacher supply. The first concerns the creation of a leadership (including middle management) structure in schools. The present lack of such an infrastructure is a significant weakness in the organisation of schools and their capacity to innovate, develop and respond speedily to emerging challenges. To remedy the lack will only be feasible if the staff involved can be freed from full-time teaching duties and additional teachers can be appointed to fill the consequential gaps in the timetable. The second concerns the necessity of training for new responsibilities. Some training can be arranged at the school level, though this still necessitates releasing staff from their regular duties. Most training, however, can only be effectively arranged at appropriate centres where school leaders from many schools can be assembled and suitable teaching and non-teaching resources can be concentrated. Replacements will be required.

Induction and in-service training

In the next chapter we shall argue in favour of the creation of a system of career-long in-service training (including a graduated period of induction) and examine the implications for training facilities and school organisation. Here it must suffice to emphasize that such a system would necessarily require a substantial improvement in school staffing levels.

The "export" of teachers

There will continue to be shortages of teachers in many fields in anglophone countries and of English teachers in other countries. In addition, it will become progressively easier for teachers trained in Ireland to obtain posts in EEC countries. We would not argue that Ireland should spend much of its scarce resources to train teachers to serve abroad, but it does fit in with tradition to export talent and some of those who leave will no doubt return to serve their own country with enhanced experience and professional experience.

Conclusions

We reiterate that it has been imperative during the last few years to pursue a policy of economic retrenchment, and that it would be improvident to relax financial constraints on the education system before the national economy is fully stabilized. But we also argued above that it would be a grave error to treat the present situation as though it precluded all consideration of desirable initiatives in the future that would entail additional expenditures. There is a teacher surplus mainly because the demand for teachers is being circumstantially choked by the combination of a high PTR and the deferment of measures to foster school improvement.

In the long term it would be beneficial to lower the PTR strictly on pedagogical as well as equitable grounds, to institute a six-year secondary cycle for all students, to lengthen the school year, to appoint more specialised teachers, to strengthen school management structures, and to put in place a comprehensive system of induction and in-service training. In the immediate term, it is urgent to provide more special instruction to disadvantaged students. The system could only benefit from improved staffing levels. Finally, the regular infusion of healthy new blood into the teaching force is essential in order to prevent its arteries from hardening.

Which institutions?

As in so many other OECD countries, Ireland has had historically two types of training institution distinguished by their structure, organisation, curriculum, duration of courses, and their professional awards:

1. Monotechnic -- single-purpose and confessional -- institutions charged with the preparation of teachers in primary schools, that is, with pupils under twelve years of age. Until 1974, when they were restyled *Colleges of Education*, they were known as training colleges.
2. *Departments of Education* within colleges or universities responsible for the preparation of teachers in secondary schools, that is, pupils over twelve years of age. Their graduates, having already obtained a degree before admission, are awarded a Higher Diploma in Education (HDE).

Students in the Colleges of Education followed a course of two years until 1974 and thereafter a course of three years. Students in the Departments of Education follow a course of one year. Teachers of vocational subjects have not been required to hold a teaching qualification but many of them have voluntarily undergone training. Since its creation in 1969, the College of Education (Thomond) has provided a four-year, purpose-designed course for students destined to teach special subjects.

The distinction between the two types of training institution has been underlined by the fact that whereas the Colleges of Education are financed by and ultimately answerable to the Department of Education, the departments of education are financed out of general university funds and their students' qualifications for teaching are approved by the Teachers' Registration Council, established in 1914. Proposals to remove the dichotomy have not been followed through, for example, to set up a common registration council - *Comhairle Mhúinteoireachta.*

Whether a short- or long-term view of teacher supply determines recruitment policy is crucial for the future size, vitality and very survival of the teacher training institutions. These underwent rapid expansion from the early 1960s as the size of their intakes complemented, more or less, the increase in school enrolment, especially at the post-school level. From the early 1980s they began to contract in order to reconcile as far as possible the size of their intakes with the number of teaching posts available. During the last few years enrolments have been in free fall, especially in the Colleges of Education. In 1986, the Minister of Education felt obliged to take the decisive step of closing one of the three big Colleges of Education. Now three options are open to the national authorities :

   i)   to maintain the *status quo*;
   ii) to close down more institutions;
   iii) to effect mergers and the consolidation of teaching and physical resources.

If a strictly short-term economic stance is adopted, it might be argued that one of the two remaining large colleges should be closed along with the few small colleges, except for the Church of Ireland College of Education which should be sustained on grounds of denominational equity. The colleges training teachers in Home Economics and Art and Design might also be reprieved since they can claim to be matching a known demand. Ireland would then be left with only one institution of appreciable size for the training of primary teachers. The choice of which of the two big colleges to close would be made according to such criteria as the level of current intakes and geographical location.

For their part, the university departments of education have greater control over their enrolments and more diversified functions than the monotechnic Colleges of Education. Moreover, their graduates have better opportunities than college graduates of finding alternative jobs outside the education system or of teaching abroad. The examiners were informed that as high a proportion of HDE graduates as 50 per cent had found alternative posts in 1987/88. Nevertheless, their principal *raison d'être* is the training of secondary school teachers for Irish schools, and it may be inferred that, on moral as well as economic grounds, they should not admit more than a small percentage of students above the number that the teaching force is anticipated to require. The small percentage surplus would allow for a little wastage and some successful students going to teach abroad or to work in para-educational fields. Still, they would be admitting far fewer students than in the past and it might be argued, therefore, that their staffing resources should be curtailed and that the number of departments should be reduced.

Given the arguments deployed under the heading "What numbers?", it follows that the examiners advise against a short-term economic strategy while also dismissing maintenance of the *status quo*. Instead, they wish to propose an alternative option viewed within a long-term perspective. Their advice is rooted in two major considerations:

i) If some or most of the present capacity for the initial preparation of primary and secondary teachers is removed, the process of recreating it in order to match the essential qualitative needs of the national education system in the years ahead will be both costly and difficult;

ii) It is urgently necessary to expand and rationalise the provision of in-service training.

The option proposed by the examiners is that of merger and consolidation. All initial training courses now lead to the award of a degree validated by a university and the students of some Colleges of Education already have access to university courses and general facilities. In short, there is already close collaboration between the monotechnic institutions and the universities. The examiners suggest that this collaboration could be formalised by merging each of the colleges with a university department of education so as to constitute a school or faculty of education. Such a measure has been adopted recently in several OECD countries and in Ireland could have the following advantages:

i) it could reinforce those practical aspects of training and help disseminate those pedagogical values that have been traditionally associated with the highly-regarded Colleges of Education;

ii) it could enrich the two types of training by offering a common core of studies and common professional preparation for those who will teach at the lower secondary as well as at the primary level. This would fit in with the general desire to see compulsory schooling designed as a continuum;

iii) it could strengthen overall educational research and development capacity;

iv) all the staff of the Colleges and departments of education could be retained but redeployed, where appropriate, according to their qualifications and major professional interests;

v) all the existing physical facilities and resources such as libraries could be shared on the model of a decentralised campus.

The arrangements for and timing of mergers and the process of consolidation would necessarily be made in the light of a detailed survey of needs and resources and with due consideration of national priorities.

The existing training institutions are potentially the only sure guarantee of a high-quality system of in-service training organised in conjunction with support programmes for the schools in the form of detailed curriculum development and teaching and learning resources. In our view, much of their attention and a substantial portion of their resources should be redirected to that end. How this is accomplished is critical for the future well-being of Irish education. If it is treated as an expedient to minimise the downturn in initial teacher training programmes, the nation and, eventually, the very programmes themselves will be the losers. The all-important reason for expanding and rationalising the national provision of in-service training is to maximise the effectiveness of the instruction given in schools.

Finally, pre-service and in-service teacher training programmes are essential components of professional institutions that have responsibility for research and community activities. Suitably integrated, practitioner programmes in Education, as in Business Studies, Engineering or Medecine, can help define and diagnose educational needs and make research findings more relevant.

NOTES AND REFERENCES

1. *Submissions*, p. 14.
2. *Submissions*, p. 335.
3. *Ibid., passim*. Almost every person or group interviewed by the examiners referred at some point to the exceptional quality of primary school teachers.
4. See Commission of the European Communities, *The Conditions of Service of Teachers in the European Community* (Brussels, 1988) pp. 133 FF. The examiners heard surprisingly few complaints about salaries from any source. The only group who appear somewhat dissatisfied are lay school principals who point out that the gap between their salaries and those of classroom teachers is much too narrow to compensate for the demanding nature of their duties.
5. For example, the following comment is based on an analysis of all the OECD educational policy reviews up to 1978: "A second issue has been... that of teacher supply. The background reports do not show the astonishingly volatile (*sic*) movements to which the various countries have been subjected. Some time before the 1967 review, the Swedes were predicting a surplus of teachers as occurred in 1971/72. Now, however, when other countries certainly do experience a surplus, there is a shortage in some of the urban parts of Sweden". (Kogan, M., *Education Policies in Perspective: an Appraisal* (OECD, Paris, 1979).
6. OECD, *The Teacher Today*, 1990: "...the determinants of teacher supply and demand embrace a complex web of factors beyond those most well-publicised of, on the supply side, salaries and, on the demand side, demographic developments" (p. 53);
"...adjustments of behaviour and policy have in the past proved the direst warnings to be exaggerated and the future simply holds too many unknowns", (p. 64).
7. *Submissions*, p. 226.
8. See OECD, *The Teacher Today, op. cit.*, pp. 22-24.

9. See, for example, Karweit, N., *The Organisation of Time of Schools: Time Scales and Learning* (Johns Hopkins University, 1978); Smith, W.J., "Time and School Learning" in Postlethwaite, T.N., and Husèn, T. (eds.), *International Encyclopedia of Education*, p. 5271: "...the large number of studies that have pursued the connection between pupil engaged time and achievement, have established remarkable consistency between pupil engagement and achievement-related outcome measures of learning. This appears to be so for a variety of pupil ability levels, grade levels, and curriculum areas".
10. U.S. Department of Education, *What Works* (Washington D.C., 1987).

Chapter 7

THE TEACHING CAREER: TRAINING AND INCENTIVES

The multiple roles of teachers

The bulk of the written submissions to the examiners directly addressed the teaching role and the nature of the education and training that the teacher receives or ought to receive. These matters also featured most prominently in our site visits and interviews. We have also studied the several substantial reports that have been published on various aspects of the condition of teachers and teaching. It is not surprising, therefore, that a vast array of expectations of the teaching profession and attributes of the adequate or good teacher have been put forward.

Teachers' roles, as presented to us, must encompass not only the instructional, the custodial, the inspirational, and the disciplinary but extend into practically all spheres of life with teachers acting as agents of physical, moral and spiritual development, emotional and mental health, and social welfare. Among the qualities called for -- in addition to the academic and the pedagogical -- are political and negotiating competence, accountancy and fund-raising abilities, a repertoire of skills to assume extra-curricular responsibilities and to communicate with widely diverse groups, planning and management skills, and an up-to-date knowledge of developments in technology and working life. Evidently, G.B. Shaw was right: the teacher would have to live to the age of Methuselah in order to accumulate all the knowledge and professional expertise required to do the job properly. An urgent requirement is to determine priorities in the teacher's tasks and to examine the possibilities for greater role differentiation within the profession of teaching. Lacking them, teacher education and training will always seem to fall well short of the multiplicity of demands being thrust upon teachers.

The teaching career, like that of other professions, extends, if not over Methuselah's aeons, then for many practitioners over several decades. It is our basic contention in this chapter that the education and training for this career should be continuing and not seen simply as a preparation for and introduction to it. This entails creating a framework in which the elements of induction and in-service play a role at least as vital as that of initial training.

Education and training for what?

In the preceding chapters, we have offered our interpretation of the wider educational scene in Ireland, highlighting the strength it has attained by virtue of the calibre of its teaching force. We have at the same time raised what we perceive as the fundamental questions and issues facing the education authorities in the unremitting effort to provide an appropriate form of education for all young people, to make the most beneficial use of resources and to improve the quality of the education received. In this chapter, we turn to the central importance of teacher education and training.

Teacher education and training do not function independently of the overall operations of the school system. Systematic knowledge derived from research and scholarship and direct experience of those operations provide its main foundations. Educational scholarship today is broad, incorporating studies and interpretations of a wide range of human endeavours and drawing upon a considerable array of disciplines, both scientific and philosophical. In Ireland, the majority of the staff in teacher training institutions are former school teachers who have made a systematic study of the educational disciplines and are themselves among the best informed and most authoritative leaders of educational thought thanks to their practical experience of the school system, and their research and scholarship. They maintain continuing links with the schools and shoulder a dual responsibility to the practice of schooling and to the subject of education in all of its ramifications.

The content of teacher education has undergone many changes in recent years and is closely attuned to school life. Although physically separate, schools and other parts of the education service are usually directly or indirectly involved in major decisions over course content and organisation, especially in the areas of teaching practice and pedagogical methods for initial teacher education and training. Despite this collaboration and the efforts made by teacher educators to keep in touch equally with school and academic life, there is a recurring worry that the colleges and departments of education will become isolated. That is why, in some countries, it is a requirement that teacher educators regularly teach in schools or otherwise actively engage themselves in school life.

One of the basic issues to be considered in Ireland is the extent to which present national education policies and arrangements facilitate the close interaction that is needed between the activities of the school, the programmes and practices of the teacher education institutions and the wider cultural, social and economic environment. Teacher education and training should not be singled out but, like all other education sub-systems, taken into account whenever new developments in education are afoot.

As a joint enterprise of colleges and universities, schools, the wider profession and the public authorities, they should feature in all major reforms and experimental programmes. It is not so much that their content and process will necessarily be revised with every major policy shift, or that they should faithfully reflect and follow school practice since elements of that practice are themselves problematic and teacher education, rightly conceived and organised, can materially assist in their improvement. Nor is it merely a question of ensuring that, within an overarching policy framework, the basic elements of curriculum, pedagogy, school organisation, resources, teacher supply and teacher education are harmonized, although that, too, is a requirement which has been signalled in the preceding analysis. The key prerequisite is the more pragmatic one of ensuring sound working relationships and interactions among the hundreds of schools and the institutions training and educating teachers, as well as a number of other institutions and agencies participating directly in in-service programmes.

It is necessary to develop a broad policy framework for teacher education and training and to promote the innovative role of colleges and departments of education. Within this framework, relations among the policy-makers, the providers and the teaching force need to be close and positive. Teacher education, like teaching in schools, has a variety of roles. Since the range is potentially vast, priorities are accordingly called for. It is essential, above all, to recognise the absurdity of trying to achieve in the initial phase of teacher education and training a level of competence, skill and understanding among teachers that properly belongs to a lifelong education and training regime.

The starting point for a comprehensive scheme of teacher education should not be an initial course as a discrete preparation for entry to the profession. Instead, in common with other professions, teaching must be perceived as a career. Professional development is best conceived and planned with regard to the different phases and stages of that career. Decisions are required, by individuals and by the education authorities at all levels, about the kinds of educational and training opportunities that are appropriate within a career-long perspective.

The concept of continuing teacher education is not a new one, but its formulation is still at a rudimentary stage in Ireland as in most other countries. Many implications have to be considered and widespread consultation and discussion will be required.

To begin with, instead of regarding in-service professional development as an optional and voluntary *ad hoc* experience, all educators and the community should perceive it as normal and, in a sense, ordinary. Such an approach requires a reversal of the present way of looking at teacher education and training, with so much of official attention and resources confined to:

a) The initial three or four-year phase of concurrent or consecutive education and training, usually entered immediately after the prospective teacher leaves school;

b) Various short and usually specialised in-service courses and programmes to meet specific, emerging needs, for example the use of computers in classrooms, discipline problems, or school-industry liaison, or to overcome specific teacher shortages in science, modern languages, and other subject areas. The long-established pattern of summer schools conducted by the inspectorate has been perhaps the principal vehicle for these kinds of courses.

The initial phase

In the previous chapter, we drew attention to the distinction between the functions and organisation of the Colleges of Education and the university departments of education. The structure and nature of the training are also different. Students in the former study discrete subjects and educational theory while also practising teaching in the classroom. Known as the concurrent model, this is seen to be process-oriented and concentrated on classroom pedagogy. Students in the latter, after obtaining a university degree, study educational theory and also practise teaching in the classroom. Known as the consecutive model, this is seen to be content-oriented, that is, the main objective is the acquisition of subject knowledge in breadth and depth. It has always been commonly assumed that the graduates of the colleges were equally well-grounded in teaching methods and in content, whereas the graduates of university departments were much stronger in content than in methods. The subject and educational theory components of the college courses were greatly reinforced from 1974 when the old two-year course was extended to three years and students became eligible for a B.Ed degree. This was a major turning point in the evolution of teacher training and a belated recognition of the inadequacy of a two-year course. The formal divide between the universities and the colleges was also reduced as the former became responsible for validating the new degree.

However, the distinction remains considerable. The colleges are not funded to undertake research and have no post-graduate programmes. By contrast, university departments of education regard research as an essential function and offer a large number of post-graduate courses, including a variety of diplomas as well as M.Ed, M.A., and Ph.D. degrees. As already pointed out, another distinction is that the colleges of education must not exceed a certain quota of entrants whereas the departments are not similarly restricted. In practice, the departments belonging to the constituent colleges of the National University observe an open access policy whereas two colleges select their entrants.

As in other countries, the merits and demerits of concurrent and consecutive courses have been exhaustively debated over many years. Concurrent courses are said to permit the marriage of theory and practice from an early stage and to acquaint students with the disciplines of education over three years rather than a single year. The consecutive model is generally acknowledged to be less satisfactory in respect of professional training needs. The one-year post-graduate course is necessarily overcrowded but still does not allow sufficient time either for the study of educational disciplines or for teaching practice. It is a model, however, that fits in with the wider concerns of universities and the convenience of undergraduates, who can choose to take up a teaching career towards the end rather than at the beginning of their degree programme. The universities favour the consecutive model because it ensures an annual flow of students into subject areas that might otherwise be under-subscribed. Indeed, during the years of secondary school expansion, a large number of undergraduates had a teaching career in view, especially in the arts and humanities, from the beginning of their studies.

One obvious way of improving the efficacy of the consecutive model, advocated by some educationists, would be to extend the one-year diploma course to two years. An additional year would certainly allow considerably more room for studying the disciplines of education and for teaching practice. On the other hand, it might act as a deterrent to those would-be teacher candidates averse to facing two years of professional training on top of a complete undergraduate course. More importantly, it would have expensive financial implications for the education authorities.

The examiners believe that, leaving aside the cost factor, it would be inadvisable to transform the diploma into a two-year course on the grounds that the gain in the quality and intensity of the professional preparation would not warrant it. In their view, it would be preferable to lengthen and reinforce the process of induction into full-time teaching perceived as an integral part of initial teacher preparation. Within such a perspective, the departments of education would continue to have some responsibility for the professional development of their graduates up to the termination of the induction period. Another option would be to offer courses in the educational disciplines as part of ordinary degree programmes.

One institution, Thomond College of Education, offers a four-year course organised according to the concurrent model. The college staff, not surprisingly, attest to its success, usually in glowing terms. There are some staff members of the departments of education who also favour the concurrent model if only in principle. In actuality, it is not a realistic option for them.

The examiners have not reached any definite conclusion about the relative merits of concurrent and consecutive approaches except to say that both have their place and are meeting real needs. Concurrency orientates students more quickly to the teaching career, maintains interactions between academic and professional studies and teaching practice over a longer period than does consecutive training, and gives students more direct experience of school life. Consecutive training, on the other hand, is built on the principle of a high degree of subject specialisation, which is necessary for teaching in many second level schools and, potentially at any rate, broadens the opportunities for student career choice while at the same time providing a solid foundation for educational and pedagogical studies. The two approaches should be seen as complementary rather than competitive. That there are differences in the length and the constituents of the two programmes need not cause concern when both are viewed within the framework of induction and continuing in-service education. The university courses would benefit from more extended periods of teaching practice, although organising them could prove very difficult. College courses might allow more scope for high-level academic work, although we acknowledge that the three-year programme is already a very full one. It would be desirable to provide a greater range of opportunities for prospective primary teachers in the consecutive programmes and for second level subject specialists in the concurrent programmes. This would be consistent with our arguments that transition arrangements between primary and secondary schools need to be improved and that steps need to be taken to foster greater continuity in curriculum and pedagogy from the beginning to the end of schooling.

The increase in the length of the initial programme for primary teachers from two to three years resulted in a recasting of curricula, with greater emphasis given than hitherto possible to educational and academic studies and a longer and more varied period of practical work in schools. But now these curricula are overcrowded and unable to provide the full range of knowledge and skills that students need. A fourth year is proposed[1]. We believe the *equivalent* of a fourth year built into the career-long development model would be preferable. Admittedly, the difference in length of training (3 or 4 years) and in its form (concurrent or consecutive) reinforce divisions between primary education and second level education that elsewhere in this report we have proposed should be reduced in a more integrated approach. But the consecutive model is not really four years of *teacher* education and to add a fourth year to the already strong concurrent programmes would in its own way contribute to a widening of the gap. The two sets of four years would not be comparable. For other reasons, too, we believe that teacher education and training should be more closely linked with the practice of teaching[2]. So our preference is for interspersing, throughout the teacher's career, periods of full- and part-time education.

Courses in the departments of education conform to a standard pattern, mingling theory and practice through four elements:

-- The disciplines of Education;
-- Teaching methods;
-- Elective courses;
-- Teaching practice.

Students are required to complete at least 100 hours of teaching practice during the school year, but most spend considerably more hours in a school placement up to a total of 300. One department requires 300 hours of school attendance and a minimum of 140 hours of teaching practice. The trainees are supervised by teachers in the schools working on a part-time and voluntary basis. The great importance attached to the practical components is demonstrated by the long-established custom of restricting lectures, seminars and other non-teaching activities to the afternoons and evenings. Incidentally, the examiners were struck by the fact that the university departments of education have no right to place students in schools. The optional character of school placements in secondary schools bears looking into.

One controversy with regard to the preparation of secondary school teachers concerns their previous academic studies rather than their professional training as such. In order to become eligible as teachers, undergraduates are expected to master three subjects. The arguments for and against studying several subjects at the university level are well known. There are those who believe that only one subject or a combination of a major and a minor subject can be mastered in sufficient depth and breadth to equip a teacher for effective performance, certainly at the upper secondary level. In other words, a general degree is not sufficiently demanding or, conversely, too demanding and therefore diluted[3]. Others argue that three subjects can be adequately mastered. What is certain is that teachers capable of dealing with three subjects can be deployed more flexibly than teachers capable of dealing with only one or two. This consideration carries particular weight in a country where there are so many small secondary schools that cannot afford to support a team of single-subject or two-subject specialists and where the intake of new teachers has been reduced to a bare minimum.

We visited nearly all the initial education institutions and were impressed with the quality and commitment of their staffs, the strength of the programmes and the standard of buildings, teaching spaces, laboratories, equipment and other facilities now generally available. Despite the pressures, initial teacher education is already of a good and appropriate standard and, happily, the means very largely exist at present for the further development that should and will undoubtedly occur. Most important, the quality of the teacher educators is high. The reforms of the 1970s and the injection of resources for capital works, equipment and staffing, have provided a foundation upon which to continue to build. Thus, a well organised, effective and professionally and academically sound structure for initial teacher education already exists. Improvements such as a greater injection of practice, especially in the university (consecutive) programmes may be difficult but they are achievable.

In Chapters 3 and 4 we have suggested that further consideration should be given to a number of quite specific aspects of primary and secondary schooling. For each of these, there is a challenge for initial teacher education. But the challenge cannot simply be met by adding yet further elements to an already overcrowded teacher education curriculum. There have been many quite substantial improvements in the curriculum of teacher education in recent years and these have generally been achieved by thoroughgoing reappraisals. The colleges and departments of education have shown themselves well able to undertake such reappraisals and to modify their programmes accordingly.

The rationale for career-long education and training

The challenge that now faces the authorities and indeed the whole teaching profession is how to address in a comprehensive way the needs and aspirations of talented and well-educated young teachers as they make their first full-time professional encounters with the school (induction) and as they progress through their careers (continuing in-service education and training). We believe that the best returns from further investment in teacher education will come from the careful planning and construction of a nationwide induction and in-service system using the concept of *the teaching career* as the foundation. We say "teaching" to emphasize the point that steps must be taken to ensure that Ireland's excellent teachers stay in the classroom and gain satisfaction from doing so. At the same time, the model we propose includes in-service education for principals and other persons concerned with the education service in addition to the classroom teacher.

There is no dearth of potential expertise for induction and in-service purposes within the system, whether in the universities and colleges, the inspectorate, the professional associations and unions and in the schools themselves; nor is there any lack of willingness or enthusiasm to apply it. Ireland undoubtedly has the human capability to build up an outstanding continuing education and training system for all its teachers. We were struck by the widespread agreement about the need to set long-term targets apparent in a very large number of submissions and in our discussions around the country.

The main difficulty is not the lack of personnel but of structures on an appropriate scale and with the required scope of provision and access. The structures are lacking, partly because of the ever-present constraint of limited resources, and partly because the detailed policy planning required to establish them nationally has yet to be undertaken. The 1984 Report of the Committee on *In-Service Education* went some way towards indicating how such plans might be prepared through a new national body but this has not been established and there is a lack of co-ordination at the levels of both policy and provision. There is, moreover, no agreement on whether in-service education shall remain voluntary (as the *In-service Report* recommended) or become a requirement. We take the latter view and would support the linking of the credential to teach to the meeting of specific in-service demands. It is this pattern that we believe will become widely established in many professions in the future.

Before coming to the kind of framework that, in our view, will make a major contribution to teacher education, it is necessary to consider the rationale of what would be, in practice, a substantial national commitment, with considerable resource implications. Just how important are induction and in-service programmes and what will be achieved if measures can be taken to enhance and strengthen the present provision?

The first and foremost requirement is to ensure that the present high standards of entrants to the teaching profession are sustained and that the motivation and commitment of teachers are kept alive throughout their careers. Of the procedures potentially available, salary enhancement, performance and merit awards, improved pupil/teacher ratios and other benefits directed at the working conditions of teachers should all be considered, controversial though some may be. They entail consultation and careful negotiation with the unions and the employers.

Notwithstanding, or perhaps because of their interest in improvements in working conditions, it seems evident that most teachers are characterised by their expertise in and dedication to the profession of teaching. Consequently, they seek rewards intrinsic to teaching itself and related to their own professional advancement as teachers rather than administrators, organisers or academics. The continuing enhancement of teacher professionalism, on a career-long basis, may be the surest, although not the only, way of sustaining the commitment and standards of teachers.

A further consideration is that changes in curriculum, pedagogy and school organisation must be reinforced by new insights and skills within the teaching profession. It is commonplace, moreover, that technological and other changes in the wider environment are constantly introducing new opportunities and possibilities for teaching. Indeed, if they are not reflected in school life, the school itself will progressively lose touch with society at large and jeopardise its capacity for preparing youth for a rapidly changing world. This is the so called "efficiency gap" to which attention was drawn in the investment studies in the 1960s. The need to address it is even more urgent today.

The foregoing changes are not only technical in the realm of equipment and facilities. The content of school education must itself continue to relate to developments in human knowledge and understanding which, on all fronts, is constantly advancing. There is often a mismatch between these developments and teacher knowledge, which may mean that the teacher's knowledge is dated or that there is an inadequate supply of teachers in the new subject areas already mentioned.

Not only is the content of the established subjects changing but new themes and areas require attention. In recent years, these have included health education, environmental education and transition from school to work among others, In order to be able to handle such complex themes effectively and integrate them in an already full curriculum, teachers now in service must undergo further training.

Opportunities to keep the school attuned to contemporary life must, of course, be seen in the perspective of the core subjects and subject areas of the curriculum. We are not suggesting that teachers need episodic bursts of "updating" and "broadening" to meet every new development. Nevertheless, it is obvious that unless teachers are systematically provided with the opportunity to keep up to date with the kinds of developments that have been outlined in the preceding paragraph, education in the schools will suffer from formalism and the kind of superficiality that results from obsolescent knowledge and ideas being transmitted through routine practices. The argument that updating can be adequately assured by the individual and voluntary efforts of teachers or through nationwide syllabuses, texts and other materials prepared by relatively small groups of experts for use by the whole teaching force has been advanced. These approaches have proved quite inadequate, however, when tried and tested. In any case, in Ireland it is desirable to break away from an undue reliance on "the text", and to capitalise on the education, the standards and the professionalism of the teachers themselves.

Finally, there is the problem of injecting new blood into the teaching profession. Even if it were thought feasible to use young teachers employed on short-term contracts as a principal source of new ideas -- and we certainly do not see this as a tenable solution -- there would still remain large numbers of full-time career teachers in permanent positions whose professional knowledge and skills require systematic updating. In other words, significant improvements over the next decade in the education of the young in Ireland must rely ultimately on changes in the behaviour of already trained teachers.

Ireland has been fortunate to maintain the quality of its teaching force. Conditions now exist that make it possible to initiate policies and strategies for in-service education designed to ensure that schools can play their full part in social, cultural and economic development.

Teacher induction

We have indicated that there are two main elements in the post-initial education and training of teachers: induction and continuing professional development. Induction refers to the period immediately following completion of initial training and is limited to a specified period. The needs for this period can be defined with reference to the general question of joining a profession and the specific question of teaching and otherwise being engaged in the affairs of a single institution. There are thus general elements, which can be seen as a continuance of the broad approach of initial training but conceived from the standpoint of a working practitioner, and specific elements related to the particular characteristics of the school in which the young teacher is working. During this period of induction, the teacher may be on probation.

Thus, there is an additional requirement, that of confirming the young teacher's suitability to join the teaching profession based on a recommendation by a member of the inspectorate.

Induction is the link between the fully professional and largely self-directed role of the teacher and the preparatory, guided phase of pre-service education and training. It is of critical importance not only in orientating the new teacher to the profession but in maintaining continuity between the spheres of training and school life. For the linkage to work, it is therefore necessary to treat induction as a distinct and discrete phase in the professional development of the teacher with its own clearly-spelt out objectives, procedures, role definitions and resource allocations. Thus, for example, it must be decided whether -- and if so how -- members of the inspectorate are to be involved, other than as assessors of probation. The present duties and responsibilities of inspectors are so onerous as to make it impossible for them to make any significant contributions, over and above their role in confirming probation. Similarly, since induction must be treated as a formal part of the responsibilities of senior staff, it must be built into the definition of their role and provided for in staffing profiles, teaching loads and in salaries.

The Irish authorities, like many others, could continue with the present *ad hoc* and incomplete arrangements. Our argument is that induction should be part of a coherent pattern of the professional career and regarded as an essential component of a policy for maintaining the quality of schooling and of teachers.

Professional development of teachers in service

The approach to in-service education as a whole must be on a different basis from that applying to induction. Whereas induction by definition occurs at the beginning of the teacher's career and should be completed within a finite period and with reference to a relatively limited set of objectives and requirements, the concept of in-service education addresses the total teaching career in all its variety and extending over perhaps four decades. Whereas there can and should be a national policy framework whereby various forms of in-service education for every teacher become both a right and a responsibility, the actual provision will vary enormously in both content and form. For example, we believe that every teacher, at regular intervals, should demonstrate that he or she is maintaining active contact with the relevant subject disciplines or areas of knowledge and experience underpinning the act of teaching. We also believe that, at regular intervals, every teacher should satisfy certain performance criteria in relation to the processes of teaching and learning. There is also need for a close inter-relationship between the goals of educational reform and changing teachers' roles which can only be cemented by universal provision of well-focused in-service education.

None of these requirements is easily met, not only because of the resource demands which can nevertheless be quantified (and in turn "rationed" according to available resources), but also because the two requirements entail judgements and preferences over which there is not necessarily agreement within the teaching profession itself. But these are insufficient reasons for not proceeding to develop policies and strategies, given that practically every individual or organisation that addressed the subject in the course of our enquiry underlined the urgency of strengthening this aspect of teacher education. It is upon consensus over need that the foundations of a system-wide policy can be firmly laid. Moreover, it should not be thought that moves in this direction are confined to teaching; increasingly, in every profession, it is coming to be recognised that initial qualifications are not adequate for a lifelong career and that even the credential to practice must be renewed periodically.

It is sometimes assumed that the expression "in-service education and training" refers to short and intensive courses and programmes provided by experts external to the school, usually in non-school settings. There is, of course, a place for this kind of approach in such domains as information technology, major developments in subject fields and areas not traditionally taught in schools, and the findings of educational research and evaluation. There are, however, many aspects of educational development which are best approached from the perspective of the school itself and by practising teachers. For example, curriculum planning and development, pupil assessment and innovations in pedagogy should not be undertaken or disseminated without direct teacher participation. Such participation is on the one hand an example of practitioner contribution to educational development and, on the other, a form of in-service education for the participants.

We wish to emphasize the value of this latter approach and in doing so to draw attention to difficulties in school-focused or school-based in-service education, namely, the planning and utilisation of school buildings and equipment and the organisation of the school day. Traditional practice has been predicated by a model of education as a form of instruction whereby qualified adults purvey their knowledge and expertise to the young and unqualified. The partial validity of that concept must not obscure from view the fundamental transformations in the educational process that we have been discussing in this report. In particular, the need for the school to be seen as a learning institution for all of its members, teachers as well as students, must be underlined.

We have already commented in Chapter 4 on the generally unimaginative and inflexible way in which the school day is organised. In relation to in-service education we must point up the limitations of a school day model which in general totally ignores the professional development needs of the teachers themselves. As a consequence, in-service education is normally viewed as something extra that has to be provided over and above the normal teaching day, week or year. On this basis it will always be to a degree marginal for many teachers, and those participating in in-service programmes will do so very often at the inconvenience or with the forbearance of their colleagues. It is a corollary of accepting the necessity of lifelong teacher education that the very model of schooling and its organisation needs to be reconstituted.

Teaching and the knowledge base

In our short time in Ireland we witnessed solid, professional teaching, generally inspired by evident affection between teacher and students. Like much "good" teaching in Western nations, however, it was primarily didactic in nature[4]. In this form of instruction classrooms are autonomous, the teacher is the primary initiator, the students generally work alone, and the lessons are structured around content that is largely factual. We did not see any examples of small group problem-solving, team teaching designed to free teachers for special work with students having learning difficulties, or the use of computer or video technology to support instruction, although we do not doubt that examples are to be found in some schools.

Without question there can be great merit in the traditional "didactic" model. Scholastics throughout the centuries have practiced it effectively, and it is the pedagogy of choice for colleges and universities throughout the world. Resourceful and clever students who have the motivation to learn can profit from articulate, well-structured, didactic lessons.

But current research on teaching and learning clearly indicates that reliance on didactic instruction alone will not accomplish the tremendous educational tasks that lie ahead. To prepare all students to be productive in the society of the year 2000 will require schools and teachers that actively involve students in the learning process, as well as a pedagogy and content that are integrated, challenging, and sensitive to differences in individual learning styles[5].

This conclusion, and our overall approach to improving the effectiveness of instruction, are drawn primarily from research in four main areas[6]:

i) the student learning process: how do students process, integrate, remember and use new information?
ii) the teaching process: what are effective strategies for facilitating student learning and what do teachers need to know in order to use these strategies effectively?
iii) the management and structure of schools: what characteristics of schools create an environment for effective teaching and learning and can such an environment be generated?
iv) testing: can assessment/testing procedures be developed that both ensure accountability and promote desired learning objectives?

Underlying much of the current research is a cognitive conception of the act of learning -- that is, learning is a process of constructing and reconstructing meaning. This view differs from previous conceptions in several key respects. Most importantly, it sees learning as requiring *active involvement* on the part of the learner. No longer can the student be regarded as a passive recipient of new information. In addition, this approach draws no sharp distinction between "lower order" and "higher order" learning tasks. Instead, cognitive learning theorists today argue that all students should be challenged with problems requiring "higher order" thinking, given their current level of understanding and skill. Finally, the cognitive conception of learning assumes no single learning strategy or mode but rather recognises that individuals differ considerably in the ways they process, assimilate, and remember new information.

This view of learning has a variety of implications for teaching. Above all, it implies that the role of the teacher is not primarily to present facts for drill and practice but to create active learning opportunities for students. Some of these opportunities may be in the form of didactic instruction, but many may not. For example, given the learner's need for active involvement and for "higher order" challenges, both "hands on" conceptions of science instruction and the use of co-operative learning situations would appear appropriate and useful. This fact underscores the need for flexibility in school organisation and for well-prepared teachers.

After 30 years of research on teaching (including studies of teacher beliefs and behaviours) the current conception of teaching is that, while it is complex and difficult, there are some understandable processes that distinguish good from mediocre and bad teaching. Most of this research is focused on the process itself, with some more recent exploration into teaching of specific content areas. Four bodies of recent research require attention.

Process-product research emphasizes "active instruction", maximisation of learning time, and structured presentation of content. Good teaching in Irish schools fits the findings of this research. Good active instruction is especially effective for teaching skills and factually-based material.

Research on holistic instructional strategies has focused on the examination of various instructional strategies, such as open classrooms, individualised instruction, and mastery learning. Particularly promising is the research on structured student interactions, including peer and cross-age tutoring and co-operative learning. These approaches build on findings of process-product research but utilise other students rather than just teachers. They are also more congruent with recent research on learning than individualised instruction and mastery learning, which are based more on behavioural learning theory and hierarchical curricula. There is a strong literature showing positive results for both low- and high-achievers for the use both of co-operative learning and peer and cross-age tutoring. However, these strategies are often difficult to implement and require flexibility in classroom and school organisation.

Recent research on individual differences and the needs of disadvantaged students indicates that:

i) Effective teaching should emphasize both lower-order and higher-order skills for all learners. This is especially important for low-achieving students, who may have more difficulty developing higher-order thinking on their own.

ii) The *quality* of time devoted to learning is often more important for low-achieving students and for higher-order learning than is quantity of time.

iii) *Direct* instruction, which seems to be particularly effective for low-achieving students, is a necessary but not sufficient method for teaching higher-order skills to any student -- it needs to be combined with more open-ended strategies in order to foster knowledge construction.

iv) Students should have the opportunity to participate in small heterogeneous ability groups, which can foster achievement, motivation and social development. The literature indicates that schools should not isolate low-ability students in homogeneous groups so as to avoid fragmentation of skills. Low-ability children seem to need particular help in drawing connections between different pieces of information and skills.

There is a growing body of research *on content-based teaching strategies* linking the teaching process with the content of instruction:

i) Teachers need both breadth and depth of subject-matter knowledge to be effective in their instruction.

ii) Teachers need to know how to convey this knowledge -- pedagogical strategies should be linked to specific content areas in order to aid students' construction of meaning.

What are the policy implications of research on teaching? The research underscores the importance of extensive teacher preparation and continuing in-service education in the integration of subject matter and pedagogy. Prospective and serving teachers need continually to build and rebuild their repertoire of effective strategies, expand their knowledge base, and develop and redevelop effective pedagogical theories. At the school level, the research suggests the importance of teacher flexibility and responsibility in making pedagogical decisions. To meet the varied needs of students and to be able to use a broad range of strategies, teachers must be able to count on a flexible and supportive school organisation.

Ways and means

We have sketched an approach to teacher education which assumes a career-long model. While co-ordinated national planning and resourcing are needed if this is to be achieved, the delivery of teacher education must involve a large and varied array of agencies. The colleges and universities already participate in all phases of teacher education and could undertake additional responsibilities for induction and in-service, if supported to do so. The provision of advanced diploma courses in special educational fields, and courses leading to post-graduate degrees should be strengthened, and consideration should be given to aiding teachers who attend such courses. The existing network of teacher centres should be expanded and strengthened to provide regionally and locally accessible facilities for meetings and practical projects. The professional associations and unions have an important part to play as also do such bodies as the associations of managers and parents.

Earlier in Chapter 3 we considered the overall role of the inspectorate and recommended that they abandon their direct responsibility for organising in-service training courses. Here we wish to emphasize the importance of their role in improving the quality of teaching and the administration of schools through professional development of school staff. First, they can serve as a continuing source of information and advice for teachers and principals about the nature and content of curriculum and other requirements placed on the schools by the Department. This is an especially critical function for small and rural schools. Second, as part of their task of monitoring the performance of new teachers, they can provide systematic guidance.

We have argued earlier for increasing the capacity of the Inspectorate so that they can monitor schools more effectively. The argument for increasing capacity is even stronger in the context of helping to make schools and teachers work better. We have also suggested that there should be some decentralisation of the functions of the Ministry. Our view is that this would be particularly helpful in improving the functioning of the Inspectorate.

A policy for career-long education and training should be essentially similar for all categories of teachers. At present, the rules are different for primary and seconday teachers. Primary teachers can benefit from three days of leave during the year following attendance at a one-week recognised course held during the summer period. At secondary level, however, INSET is voluntary and must be taken up outside school hours during the school year. Vocational teachers may be required to attend courses from time to time. When teachers attend certain INSET courses provided by universities they have to pay for them without tax deduction.

In relation to this issue, two recommendations in the 1984 Report of the Committee on In-Service Education are open to question:

i) The practice of offering one term of INSET every 5 to 10 years might be too rigid to cope with the number and variety of training needs over the years ahead. It also runs counter to the idea that INSET is a permanent feature of professional development;

ii) The idea of retaining the principle of *voluntary participation* also runs counter to the necessity of ensuring that any teacher who needs training in order to perform at an acceptable level of professional competence should be required to attend a suitable course.

New incentives for teachers to attend INSET courses on a regular basis are evidently required. Compensatory leave during the school year seems to be inadequate even if a pool of substitute teachers is created to replace teachers on leave for training.

The mobilisation of the various agencies that can contribute to INSET should be based on an appraisal of the best recent experiences, especially those developed within the vocational preparation and training programmes related to schemes funded by the EEC. Traditional modes of instruction for teachers should be rigorously updated and complemented by a major expansion of school-based INSET. Some school-based training experiments have been started at the primary level. It would be helpful to evaluate their initial impact and to build on their strong points.

A network of teachers' centres already exists, some within the established training institutions. The examiners were impressed by the work of the few centres that they visited. It is recommended that greater use should be made of them in conjunction with the courses provided by the major training institutions.

A weak element in current INSET policy in Ireland, as in nearly all OECD countries, is the lack of serious evaluation of its impact in view of its relatively high cost. It is indispensable that any national or local institutional agency made responsible for INSET should commission a systematic evaluation of programmes.

A National Council

Whether a national council is required to address the issues of teacher selection, initial training, credentialling, induction and in-service has been debated at length; the majority view in Ireland supports the idea. While such a council would inevitably widen the scope of bureaucracy and add to the number of central agencies, we do not see how teacher education is to undergo the necessary transformation that we have outlined unless some kind of centralised machinery is established. It should be statutory, reporting to the Minister of Education, and representative of a wide range of interests apart from those of the teachers themselves.

School leaders and school managers

In many OECD countries today the spotlight has turned on the role of principals (heads, leaders). If in a few countries they are still viewed as at most *primus inter pares*, in many countries they are regarded as the key agents in maintaining quality in schools and in managing educational reforms. In Ireland, the role of principal appears to be somewhere between these two positions, although several of our interlocutors described them as a greatly under-used and "under-paid" resource.

In the past, nearly all principals were clergymen or nuns. Today there is an increasing tendency to appoint laymen and laywomen. At the same time, there is a changing assessment of the nature of the principals' role as they are perceived as key agents in the educational process. Key agents, but not the key agents, for, in Ireland, the independence of individual teachers remains uncontested, and the emergence of almighty principals would seem to be highly unlikely.

Any lack of clarity about major policy directions for the future could prevent the sound preparation and adaptation of school leaders. At secondary level, school leaders are facing particular difficulties in defining their role in the management of change. The absence of detailed school tasks results in principals being unable to develop a valid basis for evaluating teacher performance. Generally speaking, those who normally hold posts of responsibility, for example heads of departments, have no control over the work performed by individual teachers.

In a situation where schools should be equipped to cope with new demands, it is regrettable that an effective middle management capability scarcely exists. It may be added that, in the long run, maintaining an undifferentiated structure of school staff detracts from the attractiveness of teaching as a career[7]. The issue of middle management in secondary schools has been historically complex; although substantial financial provision is available for responsibility posts, these posts have not been used in practice to develop a strong middle-management structure. This is a need that should be addressed.

Both levels of schooling are facing formidable problems. Principals who are required to teach because of the small size of their schools lack the time to concentrate on specific managerial duties. Those who are relieved from some or all teaching duties still do not always have sufficient time to cope with both managerial tasks and instructional leadership. Vice-principals are expected to teach many hours and cannot always assist principals by undertaking prescribed tasks. In any case, vice-principals do not generally become principals, which seems to be a waste of their experience. The examiners consider that, if school leaders are to be able to cope with an increasingly complex managerial and instructional workload, it will be necessary :

    i) to insure that they undergo at least some initial training;

ii) to offer them direct support after their first appointment, followed by regular INSET courses throughout their careers, especially when they are required to assume new duties;

iii) to issue guidelines and to set up a national advisory centre offering practical advice on how to cope with the problems arising from major reforms or specific innovations. Some countries have instituted a "telephone help-line";

iv) to provide opportunities during INSET courses, or during periods of sabbatical leave, to experience management in other sectors of society such as industry and services and in schools that have succeeded in solving complex managerial problems;

v) to develop among teachers in general an interest in middle management and to offer appropriate courses during initial as well as in-service training;

vi) to appoint teachers to posts of responsibility in the light of their competence and skills rather than on grounds of seniority alone;

vii) to develop a strategy for replacing school leaders in training;

viii) to transfer some of the clerical and bureaucratic tasks of school leaders to non-teaching staff.

In Ireland, as in many OECD countries, women are greatly under-represented as school principals despite their numerical preponderance within the teaching profession. More of them should be encouraged to seek posts of responsibility and, specifically, training in managerial skills.

The next 10 to 15 years of falling enrolments and curricular reforms will pose formidable challenges for school managers and governing boards. Given the reality of parental choice, it would appear inevitable that schools will be competing for students. This will mean that they will have to adopt techniques for advertising the quality of the instruction and physical facilities that they are able to offer. Schools, as we have argued, will also be expected to assume full accountability for their actions. All those concerned with the government and management of schools will therefore require relevant training by means of nationally- and locally-based courses.

Finally, the examiners strongly recommend the rapid promotion of courses for parents on special topics, under the sponsorship of the Department of Education, and organised either by the groups concerned, such as the National Parents Council or by teacher training institutions or teachers' centres. If the national authorities believe that community members -- including parents -- should actively participate in determining school policies without being the prisoners of professional groups in the educational field, they should adopt a positive training policy designed to cater for their requirements.

NOTES AND REFERENCES

1. It is remarkable how quickly new demands arise. As recently as 1970 the *Report on Teacher Education* published by the Higher Education Authority stated that "... the present two-year training period for primary teachers is insufficient for the adequate development of the student-teacher" (Dublin, 1970, p. 13). Now, less that twenty years later, it is seriously proposed to double the duration of primary school training to four years. The changing context of the practice of teaching was extensively discussed in OECD, *Teacher Policies* (OECD, 1976).
2. "...the teacher competency research strategy supports the need for a sound grounding in the subject matter to be taught, while the literature on teaching strategies and special populations attests to the importance of a very good command of pedagogical knowledge and techniques" (OECD, *The Teacher Today*, 1990, p. 80).
3. "...too many students with general degrees in the popular subjects proceeding in a casual fashion to the Higher Diploma in Education" (*Report on Teacher Education, op.cit.*, p. 34).
4. John Coolahan cites research which finds that there is a "strong tendency for teachers in their third and fourth years to revert to traditional, didactic teaching styles" even if they have been trained in other ways. ("A View of the Irish Educational System: Current Issues and Problems", p. 50).
5. See, for example, *Schools and Quality: An International Report*, OECD, Paris, 1989, Chapter 5.
6. For a fuller review of this research see Smith, M. and O'Day, J., "The Teacing Process: Research and Policy", *The Teacher Today, op. cit.*, Chapter 4.
7. "Improving career structures may also mean questioning the predominant practice of teachers continuing full-time, full-year right up to a fixed retirement age. For experienced teachers, more flexible combinations of classroom teaching with other roles and duties within the school, as well as possible part-time arrangements with educational administrations or other enterprises, may prove to be administratively complex but to yield beneficial results" (OECD, *The Teacher Today, op.cit.* p. 65).

Part Two

RECORD OF THE REVIEW MEETING

Paris, 30 November 1989

1. SETTING THE SCENE

Professor Skilbeck said that the principal message the examiners had sought to convey in their report, and the central issue that they hoped to hear debated, was the opportunity, not to say necessity, of embarking upon new ways of thinking about teaching and, hence, the education and training of teachers. Their report was designed to contribute to an existing process of critical reflection, which was well under way in Ireland. They had aimed to offer an objective and constructive appraisal and to assist in bringing into sharp focus actions that seemed both possible and desirable to many Irish educators in the continuing evolution of the national education system. Practically all the examiners' comments and suggestions had their echo in Ireland itself.

Their report was neither bland nor lacking in frankness. It was in places controversial. Professor Skilbeck hoped, however, that all the examiners' observations, suggestions and recommendations would be seen as essentially constructive. They did not expect agreement on all of them. After all, Irish educators themselves were in dispute over some of the fundamental issues facing schools, teachers and teacher educators. The examiners' report was offered as a contribution to the national dialogue on schooling, teaching and teacher education, a dialogue that was of international importance as well.

In her opening statement the *Minister, Mrs Mary O'Rourke, T.D.*, addressed a number of key issues raised by the examiners and brought the Education Committee up to date on significant developments since the examiners' visit to Ireland a year before. She pointed out that it was now almost a generation since the publication in 1966 of the Report *Investment in Education*, which had been prepared by the Irish Department of Education in connection with the previous OECD review of education in Ireland. That Report had been a thorough appraisal by the Department of the education system and had set the scene for fundamental changes and major developments over the next decade.

On the very subject of investment, it was worthy of note that in 1966 government expenditure on education had represented 3.7 per cent of GNP whereas for 1990 it would be 6.1 per cent. Similarly, as a percentage of net government expenditure on non-capital services, the expenditure on education had risen from 15.5 to almost 20 per cent during the same period. These increases reflected the Government's commitment to education.

The Report on *Investment in Education* had come at a time when the Irish education system was ripe for change and the seeds of change had already been sown. Policy decisions had been taken in the early 1960s to rationalise the secondary system and to provide a broad comprehensive curriculum for all pupils. At that time there were two main categories of schools: vocational, with their emphasis on practical training, and secondary, with their largely academic content. The intention had been to provide in each type of school a comprehensive curriculum so that pupils would be able to choose from a wide range of subjects appropriate to their abilities and aptitudes. To reinforce this policy the State itself had started to build a number of comprehensive schools. Secondary and vocational schools had been encouraged to pool their resources so as to widen the educational choices available to pupils in a given locality, and a policy of amalgamation had been initiated. The Intermediate Certificate Examination, up to then taken only by pupils in secondary schools at the end of the compulsory cycle, had been introduced into vocational schools. In tandem with these developments a psychological service had been established for second-level schools.

In 1967 the concept of free secondary education had been adopted leading to a massive increase in enrolments. For the first time a scheme of grants for the building and extension of schools had been introduced to assist them to cater for the increased demand and to broaden their curriculum. A new type of school, the community school, a natural successor to the comprehensive school, had been developed, again to ensure a broad curriculum for pupils of a given area but with added emphasis on the school's key position in the community. Thus, a whole new policy for secondary schools had been developed and implemented over the last twenty five years or so and the requisite physical facilities had been provided. It was appropriate that 1989 should have seen the culmination of that policy at lower secondary level with the introduction of a new common course for pupils in all types of school leading to the new Junior Certificate.

What was really important to consider was that the new policy of providing a broad, comprehensive curriculum for all had been implemented against the background of enormous increases in the number of students to be catered for at the secondary level -- from 143 000 in 1965 to 342 000 in 1988. Ireland had gone the road of giving a broad general education to secondary pupils. For example, children were not streamed into vocational or academic tracks at an early age. There were, however, somewhat different emphases from one secondary school to another -- indeed, even within the same school. The authorities were also increasingly providing alternatives for students for whom the traditional curriculum might be too difficult or unsuitable, but, by and large, a broad general education was available to all. The Minister did not foresee any major fundamental change occurring in that particular facet of Irish education, though, of course, the authorities would continue to strive for an evermore enlivening and beneficial curriculum.

At the post-secondary level, very significant changes had also been brought about. In the 1960s, this level had consisted almost entirely of the universities, comprising five colleges, and the primary teacher training colleges. A number of reports had adverted to the lack of education for technicians, apart from apprenticeships. In order to meet this need, nine regional technical colleges had been established, mainly for the purpose of providing education and training leading to qualifications for middle-level technicians. These colleges had developed very successfully as post-secondary institutions providing certificate and diploma courses. Two National Institutes for Higher Education had been established to provide degree level courses in vocational areas such as Business Studies, Engineering, Marketing, Languages, and Communications. These had proved an outstanding success, and this year full university status had been conferred upon them as the Universities of *Limerick* and *Dublin City*. It would be appreciated, therefore, that, at the post-secondary level, a whole new structure had been put in place over a relatively short period and that this, in turn, had helped stimulate very big increases in participation rates from 20 700 in 1965 to 62 800 in 1988.

In providing for such huge qualitative and quantitative improvements at the secondary and post-secondary levels, successive Governments in Ireland had demonstrated their outstanding commitment to investing in education. It demonstrated a very pro-active, rather than reactive, policy towards education.

Apart from the quantitative increase in school provision, the curriculum had been the object of review and change. The primary school curriculum had been revised completely in 1971 to make it more pupil-centred than had previously been the case. It was under review again at the present time. The curriculum at the secondary level had also been revised. During her term of office she had established the National Council for Curriculum and Assessment. The Council had drawn up new curricula in seven subjects which formed the core of the new Junior Certificate programme.

To emphasize the continually changing process in education in Ireland, the Minister pointed out that, even since the examiners' visit, some significant developments had occurred. She wished to mention briefly the Review Body on Primary Education which had been set up with terms of reference covering a wide range of issues. Its report was expected in 1990 and would lead to widespread debate on the many important facets of primary education. A more specific review of the Primary School Curriculum was also taking place: its report would appear early in 1990.

The examiners had commented on the deficient provision for foreign languages in Irish schools. The Minister said that, since their visit, certain initiatives had been taken aimed at increasing that provision. School authorities were being encouraged to introduce an additional modern language into the curriculum and funds were being provided to help them do that. Over one-third of lower secondary schools now offered more than one modern language in addition to Irish and English. The question of introducing a modern language into the primary curriculum, where pupils studied English and Irish, awaited the recommendation of the two review groups. In conjunction with its own language training initiatives, the EEC LINGUA Programme would result in an unprecedented increase in the number of young people studying, and gaining fluency, in European languages.

In both the Background Report and the Examiners' Report, a fairly exhaustive description had been given of the Irish education system. A question which arose, of course, was whether the system as described was one whose achievements would stand international comparison. Comparing one system with another and making judgements on their efficacy were notoriously difficult. For her part, the Minister could only look at the situation as she found it. The Leaving Certificate obtained at the end of secondary school was acceptable for entry to further education all over the world. Irish graduates and diploma-holders -- doctors, engineers, technicians -- had no difficulty in competing successfully for jobs abroad. The multinational companies, and there were many, who had set up in Ireland reported that one of their main reasons for doing so was the high level of skill of the educated Irish person, particularly in the technological area. A recent report by a member of the United States National Center on Education and the Economy had spoken in very gratifying terms of education in Ireland. The report referred to the very high level of basic education of the average sixteen and eighteen year-old, to "a very well educated workforce" and to the fact that "the Irish simply had high expectations for everyone". In the light of all this evidence, the Minister believed that the Irish education system and the results that it produced compared favourably with those of any country.

The Minister did not wish, however, to convey a sense of smugness or any suggestion of Ireland resting on its laurels. For example, more must be done for those who could not aspire to completing secondary schooling. As in every country, there was a significant number of children who could not aspire to becoming diplomees or graduates. These disadvantaged children needed more investment and more help, so that they could develop to their full potential. As Minister for Education, she was acutely aware of their needs. Special provision was being made for the appointment of additional teachers, remedial and otherwise, in schools serving disadvantaged areas. A fund existed out of which payments could be made to disadvantaged primary schools for the purchase of books and equipment and to encourage liaison between the school and the home. There was also a scheme at both primary and secondary level whereby school books were provided to necessitous children. The Minister would continue to provide additional resources to combat disadvantage, which would remain a major priority.

2. POLICIES, PRIORITIES, RESOURCES, PLANNING AND CONTROL

Dr. Lowe said that the first set of questions covered large issues, most of which were currently on the agenda of other OECD countries. They extended over the entire range of educational policy-making, control and management of the education system, the level of financing and the machinery for monitoring educational progress. Although the questions were easier to pose than to answer, the examiners felt that they should be addressed now in view of the forces for change described in Chapter 3 of their report.

In Ireland, policies had historically been determined on an *ad hoc* basis to cope with urgent problems or needs. Given the magnitude and variety of the current challenges facing the education system, *was any thought being given to the adoption of pro-active policies designed to set priorities over the short, medium- and longer term? What machinery existed for facilitating the making of policy and the setting of priorities?*

The Department of Education had evolved, like many another, in piecemeal fashion as new functions had been imposed upon it. It was today large by comparative international standards, complex, and seemingly weighed down by a multitude of routine administrative tasks. Some argued that there was no call for change since a small country did not require any administrative layer between a centralised ministry and individual institutions. *Had any assessment been made of the effectiveness of the Department in its present form? Might it not operate more effectively if streamlined? Would not some decentralisation of its administrative burdens not only free it for more creative and forward-looking activities but also encourage regional and local initiatives and more effective utilisation of resources?*

Ireland devoted less to educational expenditure out of public funds than most other OECD countries given the total of enrolments in the several levels of education. This was partially explained by the traditional convention whereby religious bodies contributed substantial capital and other resources and parents paid for textbooks and other costs of their children's education, even during the compulsory period. *Were the national authorities satisfied that the present level of public expenditure was sufficient in view of the following factors:*

i) *diminution of the "private" contribution and uncertainty about its level in the future;*
  ii) *the special needs of disadvantaged schools and under-achieving pupils in all schools;*
  iii) *the absence of support staff in many schools;*
  iv) *the necessity of adapting the whole education system to a high technology age?*

The Inspectorate in Ireland was a respected body, which carried out other onerous functions than individual school appraisal, despite being under-staffed. *What did the national authorities think of the examiners' suggestion that some of its functions might be shed, for example supervising examinations, and that, besides continuing to carry out school appraisals, it might concentrate on the gathering and dissemination of ideas and information -- especially giving prominence to examples of good practice -- and on publishing reports on the general state of critical aspects of the education system?* It was understood, of course, that such a change of functions would necessitate a substantial investment in the professional development of inspectors.

What measures were being taken to ensure that the appropriate statistical and other information was available whenever an educational reform was being initiated or evaluated? What arrangements existed for commissioning and coordinating educational research, development and evaluation, both within and outside the universities, in support of the policy-making, implementation and monitoring process?

The Minister said, in reply, that the examiners had adverted to measures aimed at providing a formal mechanism for the development of pro-active policies and the setting of priorities. They had suggested that a small "cabinet" or strategic planning unit might be set up in the Department or that a National Advisory Body might be established which might generate discussion on educational issues and advise the Minister on policy. The development of new policies was, of course, an ongoing activity generated by the Government and the Department of Education. She had already dealt with policy developments since the previous OECD report, which demonstrated a very pro-active approach to new policies. New initiatives were being developed as the following examples showed:

-- the setting up of the National Council for Curriculum and Assessment and introduction of the new Junior Certificate arising from that;
-- initiatives in the area of modern languages;
-- continuing development of alternative courses under the umbrella of the Vocational Preparation and Training Programme.

Nevertheless, the Minister believed that there was a case for establishing a more formal mechanism for policy development and planning within the Department. A recent survey of the Department, undertaken in conjunction with the Department of Finance, had suggested the establishment of a Planning Unit within the Department as well as the strengthening of the policy-making capacity of its line divisions. This matter was being pursued.

The examiners had rightly pointed out the Department's weakness in generating good data, which were *a sine qua non* of policy development and planning. The problem had lain in the fact that such data as were available had been collected and processed manually and could not therefore be made available either readily or in a variety of forms. However, the implementation on a phased basis of the Department's Strategic Plan in relation to the use of information technology would radically affect the collection, storage and retrieval of data. The first phase of the Examinations Computerisation Project had been completed in 1989 with the processing of examination results, the issuing of certificates, and the production of examination statistics. In 1990, it was planned to develop the system further by using the computer to process candidate entries and to produce candidate rolls for both the oral and written examinations. Planning had also started on the design and implementation of a computerised schools inventory system, on the development of a secondary enrolments data base, on the design of a new computer system -- initially for primary teachers and schools -- which would incorporate the redevelopment of the existing primary system, and the implementation of a computerised personnel system for the Department's staff. The full implementation of the Strategic Plan would result in computerised pupil, teacher and school data bases. In this way comprehensive data necessary for the review, evaluation and appraisal of existing policies and for the development of alternative policy proposals relating to educational reform would be available and would radically improve planning and administrative procedures.

The Minister said she was indebted to the examiners for focusing attention on what they considered to be necessary in terms of policy development and planning. She was particularly interested in the proposal to establish a national advisory body to generate discussion and advise the Minister. This was an important issue which required careful reflection. She intended to consider the proposal, her initial reaction being that, if such a body were to be established, it should be consultative rather than advisory.

The Department of Education had a total personnel of 830, of which 240 were professional or technical staff. The administrative/executive staff were therefore less than 600. It served an education system of around 900 000 full-time participants and over 40 000 teachers, and administered a budget of some I£ 1.3b. The salary bill for the Department itself represented only about 1.25 per cent of the total budget. In the light of these facts the Minister had been a little surprised to read that, in the examiners' view, it was large by comparative international standards. Given the highly centralised nature of the Irish education system, she would say that it was not large but, on the other hand, the criticism that it was weighed down by minutiae was valid.

It was suggested by the examiners that a system of local or regional administrative structures would alleviate the problem of dealing with minutiae. The Minister was among those who believed that the country was too small to have another layer of administration imposed between local institutions and central Government. In Ireland, there was a culture in which people considered that they should be able to approach Ministry officials or Ministers directly on matters affecting their lives. The size of the country allowed for a certain intimacy in this regard. The examiners had acknowledged in their report that there were very close and friendly relationships between school managers and principals, on the one hand, and the Department, on the other. This was a positive factor which should not be lightly set aside. She was not convinced, therefore, of the arguments made for a regional or local administrative system.

What could be achieved, however, was the devolution of responsibility for the day-to-day running of schools to the institutions themselves. The Minister was convinced that it was possible, based on good practice and unit cost analysis, to lay down centrally the criteria and norms within which institutions could be expected to operate. Within those parameters, the schools, the Vocational Education Committees (and, in turn, their schools) should be free to make their own decisions. This would relieve the overburdened Department of routine decision-making while at the same time giving a much needed measure of independence to the schools and Vocational Education Committees. That would be her approach to the problems pinpointed by the examiners.

According to the examiners, Ireland devoted less to educational expenditure out of public funds than most OECD countries given the enrolments in its schools. The Minister had previously stated that the percentage of GNP devoted to education in Ireland would be 6.1 per cent for 1990, and that the percentage of net government expenditure on education would be almost 20 per cent of the total public expenditure. The OECD Education Committee would surely agree that these were very significant figures and demonstrated a real commitment by the Government to education. Ireland's particular problem was that there was such a large proportion -- almost one-third -- of the population in full-time education that per-capita figures did not give a true reflection of that commitment.

To the question whether the national authorities were satisfied with the present level of public expenditure on education, the Minister's reply must be "no". She was constantly striving to obtain more resources. Despite the severe financial constraints she had recently secured government sanction for: additional remedial teachers in national schools; additional teachers for primary schools in disadvantaged areas; substantial increases in the provision for free books and library facilities. Substantial provision continued to be made for the handicapped and for the children of travellers. The education of the disadvantaged would continue to be a major priority for additional funding. The demographic decline, which would pose the many problems outlined by the examiners, should provide, on the other hand, the opportunity for a smaller number of children to share in the financial provision if the level of funding could be maintained at its present relative level or, indeed, enhanced.

It was timely that the examiners should raise the issue of the role of the Inspectorate. Its major role was to help school managers and principal teachers in the educational organisation of their schools, to monitor and advise on the effectiveness of the education system, to gather and disseminate ideas and examples of good practice, to advise the Minister on all of these matters and to play an active role in the development of educational policy. There was no doubt that the secondary Inspectorate was greatly inhibited in fulfilling these tasks by reason of its onerous involvement in the examinations system. The Minister leaned to the view, and she was sure many would agree, that the inspectors should play a much larger role in the area of monitoring and advising on the performance of the education system and on policy developments. As an increase in the numbers of inspectors was unlikely to occur, this might necessitate a gradual phasing out of their duties in connection with the examinations so that they could develop to a much greater extent their other tasks and duties. This was a matter which she proposed to pursue with the Inspectorate.

The *delegate of Norway* said he had the impression that the impact of the first OECD review in the 1960s and the particular commitment to planning had quickly faded. He also commented that his own country, which also had a small population, nevertheless had no fewer than 450 local authorities. The *delegate of Australia* questioned whether it was necessary at all to maintain an inspectorate. The *delegate of the Netherlands* observed that the examiners seemed to wish to divest the inspectorate of some of their functions only to overload them with others. For one thing, how could inspectors reconcile their roles as both auditors and advisers? Both the Australian and the Netherlands delegates, echoed by the *delegate of the United States*, emphasized the necessity for school-based management and evaluation rather than external appraisal, while ensuring accountability to local communities and the country at large. The *delegate of France* asked how developments at the local level were made known to, and then fostered by, the central administration. The *delegate of Italy* said that, whether a country should operate a centralised or decentralised system of education depended on its specific cultural context. Ireland was a small country and therefore not under the same compulsion to decentralise as many other countries with a homogeneous population. The *delegate of the Netherlands* thought that, to judge from the figures for expenditure cited by the examiners, Ireland was not allocating sufficient resources to education.

The *Minister* replied to the *delegate from Norway* that strategic planning had not ceased since the 1960s. How otherwise could the participation rate in secondary education have been doubled and that for post-secondary trebled? As to the questions about the Inspectorate, it had an important role to play in Ireland, though that role must now be reviewed. Perhaps the very name "inspector" gave the wrong signals; inspectors were not "snoopers" but enablers. As to the centralisation/decentralisation tension, she believed that the new Boards of Management would provide efficient control at the school level while being accountable to their communities.

Dr. Lowe invited the Minister to comment on the examiners' analysis of the role of the Department of Education and the various factors affecting the level of resources. The *Minister* replied that it was true that the Department had too many minute tasks to perform. She believed, however, that, as school Boards of Management assumed greater responsibilities, the Department would be able to shed some of its present tasks. On resources, the examiners had been right to point to the declining financial contribution of the private sector. It was her intention to continue to target resources to disadvantaged schools and pupils. There was a shortage of auxiliary staff in schools that must be remedied over time. Finally, Ireland fully recognised the necessity of adapting education to the present age of high technology and providing resources for essential technological innovations.

3. THE SCHOOLS: ORGANISATION, PRACTICE, CURRICULUM AND VALUES

Professor Skilbeck said that a wide-ranging discussion of issues related to school organisation, curriculum and values might appear to be a diversion in a report directed towards the selection and education of teachers. But teachers were being selected and educated for curricular and pedagogical development, among other roles in schools, and the schools themselves were changing in numerous ways. Indeed, there was a quandary. On the one hand, teachers must be selected and trained for schools as they were, "warts and all". On the other hand, teachers must be capable of responding to reforms in schools and initiating changes themselves. Only by a rigorous, comprehensive and thoroughly professional approach could this quandary be overcome. Teacher education required, therefore, two kinds of agenda. First, a thoroughly practical grounding to enable the teacher to understand and cope with the existing reality in schools. Secondly, and equally important, an orientation of teachers towards the complexities and subtleties of the wider educational processes in schools and society.

In their report, the examiners had tried to follow the succession of proposals for school reform that had been put forward since the 1960s. They had drawn heavily upon official reports and reviews, particularly those of the past five years or so. They had noted the establishment of new organisations and institutions, including new types of schools and, in very recent years, the setting up of a national body to be an engine for the further development of curriculum and assessment. There was, indeed, a ferment of change beneath and surrounding the placid surface of schooling.

The general conclusion of the examiners was that all the required thought and policy framing were already available. The task now was to translate proposals into action. This required firm leadership and decision-making and reappraisal of the allocation of resources of all kinds. If there were to be reforms, directions were needed and members of the wider community had to be involved. The questions of the examiners were derived, therefore, from an appreciation of what the schools had already achieved and what the country seemed to be expecting of them in the future.

Ireland seemed to perceive its schools as the principal agents of change. Yet the necessary conditions were not present in reality. For one thing there was a good deal of rigidity in the system, particularly in curricular design and innovation. *What major curricular reforms were currently taking place or envisaged with a view to matching current social and economic needs? For example, was anything being done to reconcile what had been described as the distinctive cultures of primary and secondary education?*

In common with other countries, Ireland recognised that too many schools were disadvantaged and that some pupils in all schools were under-achieving. *What steps were being undertaken to deal with this problem and what was their effect?*

Everyone agreed that examinations played a dominant role in Irish education. They helped determine the curriculum and profoundly influenced the behaviour of teachers and pupils from the last two years of the primary schools and throughout secondary education. *Were the national authorities satisfied that the examination system was serving the best needs of society at large? Had any systematic attempt been made to analyse its effects on learning outcomes, on attitudes, and on school organisation and practices?*

The existence of different types of secondary schools is formally justified on the grounds that diversity is a good thing. *Was there any empirical evidence about the merits and demerits of each type of school? Was there in all secondary schools a reasonable balance between academic and vocational and technical studies? Did all young people have the same opportunities in such a diversified system, particularly as regards acquiring the kind of knowledge and skills wanted in the labour market?*

The *Minister* wished to reiterate that two committees would shortly be making recommendations concerning the future of primary schools, and that the secondary schools were being individually affected by reforms designed to meet real learning needs. She cited the recent introduction of seven syllabuses for the Junior Certificate. Great efforts continued to be made to ensure that the secondary curriculum served pupils across the whole range of abilities. The modes of examination were currently under scrutiny. It was true that there were several types of secondary school, but it must be remembered that the curriculum was common to all.

The *delegate of Switzerland* posed three questions: what was the nature of the social demand for education? Was the trend towards a longer period of general secondary studies for all rather than a split between general and vocational studies? Was the child-centred approach generally accepted? The *delegate of Portugal* stated that it seemed as though schools, as in other countries, were expected to draw up development plans but not given the necessary resources to see them through. The *delegate of France* wished to know how school improvement was being monitored. The *delegate of the United States* inquired whether the outcomes of school plans were monitored. The *delegate of Norway* inquired about the scope and functions of the psychological service and overall support services.

The *Minister* said that the social demand was for more general education. It should be noted, however, that the line between general and vocational studies had become blurred. There had been some reaction against the child-centred approach with certain people calling for "a return to basics" and a formal examination at the age of eleven. It was true that schools required additional funds in order to implement their individual plans. Current psychological services to primary schools were clinically based but what was needed were school-based services, mediated through the teachers. The appointment of guidance counsellors to more schools than at present was a matter to be considered. Judging school success was extremely difficult. She would say that valid criteria were performance in the national examinations, and the pupil retention rate at second-level. The implementation of school plans was not monitored.

The *delegates of Italy* and *Japan* were curious about the relationship between Church and State and between denominational and non-denominational schools. The Minister replied that nearly all primary schools were denominational, but that there were many non-denominational secondary schools: all vocational schools were non-denominational. The policy of the Department of Education was to be punctillious in respecting the wishes of parents. Thus, it had approved in recent years the creation of more non-denominational primary schools.

The *delegate of Germany* asked about the policy regarding small schools. The *Minister* replied that many small primary schools remained, and that, incidentally, most of them had a pupil/teacher ratio well below the average. It was not the policy to close small schools against the wishes of parents. However, many secondary schools had been merged and the process of voluntary amalgamation was continuing.

4. TEACHER SURPLUS AND THE TRAINING INSTITUTIONS

Professor Smith said that the quantity and quality of teachers were intimately connected, but, for convenience, he wished to concentrate on the supply of teachers and the future of the teacher training institutions. Ireland was not alone in having a large surplus of teacher training capacity at the present time, mainly as the result of the sharp decline in pupil enrolments that was rapidly making its way up through the entire school cycle. The examiners had indicated the options available for addressing the situation under the rubric of rationalisation. *How did the national authorities view the phenomenon of surplus capacity and what measures, structural, financial or otherwise, were they considering for dealing with it? Specifically, how did the authorities react to the examiners' suggestion that teacher training should be consolidated under the umbrella of universities with students opting for different specialisms and preparing to teach at different levels, notably primary or lower secondary, and care being taken to preserve the best features of the traditional training of primary teachers?*

The *Minister* felt that the examiners had correctly identified as a major issue the emergence of a surplus capacity in relation to teacher training. Because of the rapidly falling birthrate, Ireland had gone in a relatively short time from a position in the late 1970s where teacher training capacity had been significantly expanded to one in the late 1980s where the projected decline in requirements was posing problems in determining the arrangements to be made in the future. Over the past five years it had become necessary to reduce teacher training capacity by closing one of the colleges for the training of primary teachers and curtailing entry to the others. The numbers entering specialist training courses for secondary teachers had been greatly reduced, and the university departments of education had significantly lowered their intake to higher diploma in education courses.

The *Minister* found herself in agreement with a great deal of what had been said in the Examiners' Report concerning the difficulty of providing accurate forecasts. As stated in Chapter 6, "even medium-term forecasts of demand are difficult to make because there are so many unpredictable factors that are likely to invalidate them."

The examiners had mentioned among these factors the fertility rate, emigration flows, and the retention rate at the post-compulsory level. Of interest in relation to emigration flows -- and here she was referring to the emigration of teachers rather than the effect on pupil numbers of general emigration patterns -- was a study commissioned by the review body on primary education which showed that even a small change in the parameters of the model, affecting, for example, the emigration of teachers to take up teaching abroad, would very significantly modify predictions about the numbers of teachers required.

The career break scheme was also a factor difficult to measure. At present, it allowed teachers leave of absence of up to five years, and some 700 teachers a year, or approximately 1.5 per cent of all teachers, were taking breaks. As the practice had been introduced only in 1985/86, it was not yet clear what proportion of teachers would eventually return to the classroom. However, allowing that some predictions must be made, the Minister acknowledged the point made in the Examiners' Report concerning the implication of taking a short-term economic stance in terms of the closure of teacher training institutions. Since the remit of the review body on primary education included consideration of demographic changes and their implications for teacher supply, she was reluctant to anticipate what it might say in regard to future teacher requirements, though she was strongly in sympathy with the examiners' opposition to any form of short-term strategy. Her view on this would be influenced, among other things, by the consideration that, as stated by the examiners themselves, teacher training capacity, if removed at this point in time, would be both costly and difficult to recreate in the years ahead. She would prefer to explore with the training institutions the possibility of diversification, using the very considerable resources and expertise in the colleges, perhaps for enhanced in-service provision or for new forms of education and training for teachers and others.

Her remarks so far had related to the imponderables, or at least to the factors in the teacher supply and demand situation over which the authorities had no control. The biggest factor over which there was some measure of control was, of course, the pupil/teacher ratio. She agreed with the examiners' questioning of "the tendency to treat blanket lowering of the PTR as the priority of priorities", and she was aware that a significant volume of research suggested that, as the Examiners' Report put it, "lowering the ratio by one or more units had no measurable effect on cognitive outcomes." However, this did not, of course, mean that every effort should not be made to reduce ratios where they were seen to be excessive, or where special circumstances demanded it. A commitment to a specific reduction of the PTR formed part of the present Government's Programme. In line with this commitment, a reduction in the primary schools had already been announced for 1990, and the ratio in schools at the secondary level was currently under consideration. Summing up, the

Minister stated that behind an emerging surplus, apparently warranting action in relation to the reduction of capacity, there lay a complex web of factors making prediction difficult and warning against hasty measures.

On training, the Minister said that she was not happy with the suggestion that there should be a common core of studies and common professional preparation for those preparing to teach at the lower secondary as well as at the primary level. It was certainly difficult to envisage that basic studies and professional preparation should be similar all the way from the infant class to the beginning of the upper secondary level. That being so, the question arose as to where there should be a break. In the Irish situation, where the great majority continued beyond the compulsory education stage, the change from compulsory to post-compulsory education did not have the significance, in terms of curriculum and methodology, which it might seem to have. In these circumstances, it would appear that the natural place to make any distinction in teacher education provision was where it lay at present, namely between primary and secondary schooling. Of course, in the context of the type of diversification of activity and programmes that she had suggested for the teacher training institutions, some of the distinctions between different types of training, and between the training of teachers for different levels of teaching, would become less significant. In addition, where institutions could co-operate in offering provision, it was likely that common courses and programme elements would be developed jointly over time. One possible form of co-operation would be in the provision of a common basic formation for both types of teacher, followed by a year or more of specialised teacher training.

The *delegate of Switzerland* inquired whether there was *a numerus clausus* on admission to teacher training institutions. He was also curious to know what happened to those who completed a teacher training course but did not go on to teaching. He further inquired to what extent newly qualified teachers could be used as itinerant supply teachers. The *delegate of Denmark* asked what were the main priorities in face of the teacher surplus. Was the choice between improving INSET or lowering the PTR? The *delegate of Luxembourg* asked whether teachers in training followed general courses which might permit them to change to another occupation later on or whether they were trained strictly as specialists?

The Minister replied that the Department of Education controlled access to institutions training primary school teachers and that the university departments of education, although free to determine the size of their intake, had curtailed admissions to reflect the falling demand for secondary school teachers. Graduates of teacher training institutions, particularly those trained for second level teaching whose basic degree was in a variety of disciplines, went into other occupations. Many women became homemakers. And, of course, many trained teachers took up teaching posts abroad. In reply to the *delegate of Denmark*, the Minister said that several options were available, including INSET and lowering the PTR, and that the policy was to be flexible in determining priorities at any given time. As to the question from the *delegate of Switzerland*, there were no supply teachers in Ireland categorised as such, but trained teachers were available to act as substitutes for other teachers who might be absent.

Several delegates adverted to the question of the PTR. The *Swiss delegate* wondered if there was not a contradiction between preparing teachers in training in the context of theories about individualised teaching and a child-centred approach when, in practice, many of them would be coping with large classes. The *Minister* repeated that the PTR was, indeed, too high. The reason was the exceptional rise in the school population during the last three decades.

At this point, *Dr. Lowe* invited the Minister to comment on the factors affecting teacher supply that had been enumerated by the examiners, but had not so far been discussed: duration of the secondary cycle; length of the school year; shortage of teachers of special subjects; the export of teachers. The *Minister* agreed that there was a problem about the length of the secondary cycle: five years was probably too short. For some time critics had been saying that many young people in Ireland were too young on leaving secondary school. On the other hand, it had to be remembered that the school cycle in Ireland was very long since most children started at the age of four. Moreover, young people were increasingly completing six secondary school years as opposed to five. As to the school year, it was shorter than in many other countries. There was no evidence, however, that pupil performance was thereby diminished. At the same time, consideration might be given to providing more INSET outside the school year. There were shortages of special subjects, not least modern languages, but measures were being taken to remedy them. As for the "brain drain" of teachers, it was not desirable but would be lessened as economic conditions improved.

Mr. Papadopoulos (OECD Secretariat) asked about the views of teachers. Were their unions displaying the same militancy as the unions in certain other countries? The *Minister* replied that the teachers' unions in Ireland were undoubtedly powerful: "they had a lot of muscle". However, there was a long tradition of good working relations between them and the national education authorities. Teacher unions were militant in regard to salaries but also strongly pressed their views in relation to the interests of pupils and conditions in schools. In reply to a question from the *delegate of Canada* concerning the relationship between research studies and the content of training, the *Minister* said that it was one of the tasks of the National Council for Curriculum and Assessment to co-ordinate research activities and to disseminate research findings.

5. THE TEACHING CAREER: TRAINING AND INCENTIVES

Professor Smith said that, because of the sharp decline in new recruits, the focus during the next decade would be on the professional development of the teachers already in service. They were faced with the challenge of improving their pupils' learning skills. A recent international study had shown that Irish pupils performed well on tests of basic knowledge, but less well when higher order skills were called for.

Professor Smith then pointed out that most OECD countries were facing the problems of how to sustain teacher morale against a context of rapid change and how to put in place a comprehensive system of professional development. *What action was being taken in Ireland to ensure teacher effectiveness and morale against a background of high pupil/teacher ratios, vanishing recruitment of new staff, and limited job mobility? What was thought of the concept of a teaching career as described by the examiners?*

There appeared to be no systematic attempt to induct new teachers into their professional role. The assessment by an inspector at the end of the first year was thorough but very seldom resulted in failure and for most individuals it was summative rather than formative. *Was any thought being given to ways and means of providing continuing support for teachers after leaving the training establishments?*

No one concerned with Irish education disputed that the amount of in-service education and training (INSET) available was grossly inadequate. Some people also strongly criticised its arbitrary content. *What were the prospects for a sharp increase in the amount and range of in-service training? Was funding an insuperable barrier? What did the authorities think of the examiners' suggestions for reorganising and reinforcing INSET, particularly the creation of a national planning and co-ordinating body, greater use of local resources and teachers' centres, development of distance techniques, and a changed role for the Inspectorate?*

In reply, the *Minister* stated that she was in complete agreement with the concept of a teaching career. There was widespread agreement about the crucial importance of induction. There were, perhaps, better arrangements at primary than at second level. In primary schools, the fact that the Inspectorate did not have responsibilities in relation to the examination system (since there were no public examinations to supervise at that level) enabled them to give more of their attention to newly-qualified teachers. There was need for reflection, however, as the examiners suggested, in relation to the role of principals and senior teachers in both primary and secondary schools in inducting newly-qualified teachers to their schools. Clarification of these roles might result in guidelines being developed for induction programmes. The contribution of the initial teacher training institutions to induction also called for consideration. In addition, the recent emergence of a teacher surplus and the effect of career break vacancies being filled on a temporary basis had meant that many newly-qualified teachers moved from one temporary job to another. All this had not helped the process of induction.

The *Minister* agreed with the examiners that teacher appraisal and effectiveness were important and sensitive issues. At the primary level, the emphasis had been consciously shifted over the past few years from the appraisal or inspection of the individual teacher to that of the school. Individual inspection was still carried out on teachers on probation, teachers whose work was said to have deteriorated or teachers who requested inspection. The latter were mainly those who aspired to promotion, and who believed that a favourable inspection report would be of personal benefit. The shift to school appraisal at the primary level should be seen in the context of the Department's strong encouragement to schools to draw up school plans which would cover curriculum planning as well as many aspects of general school policy. The articulation of school plans and systematic reviews entailed by the Inspectorate's school reports were seen as very important instruments for promoting school effectiveness and affording a basis for further development.

At secondary level, the inspection of teachers and schools had not been as extensive as that at the primary level, largely owing to staffing difficulties and the demands made on inspectors' time by the public examinations. Secondary inspectors were recruited as subject specialists, and inspection tended, therefore, to be directed towards the teaching of specific subjects in schools, with less emphasis on a "whole school approach", though a framework for what was known as "organisation inspection" *(Eagar Cigireacht)* was in place.

One of the more controversial recommendations in the Examiners' Report had concerned what might be called the performance certification of teachers. The idea of requiring all teachers to submit at regular intervals to an examination, or inspection of their knowledge and competence, offered too much stick and too little carrot. The Minister preferred to believe that, in the same way as learning must be made attractive to even the most alienated pupils, teachers must be motivated to maintain the standard of their teaching by attractive and relevant in-service provision. The maintenance of effectiveness by voluntary means of this kind were preferable, in her view, to an approach based on compulsory appraisal, and much more attainable within a reasonable time scale.

The Minister had already mentioned the introduction in 1989 of the new lower secondary cycle leading to the new Junior Certificate, the first examination for which would be in 1992. New syllabuses had been prepared in seven subjects and would be provided progressively in the other subjects of the junior cycle curriculum. The OECD

Education Committee would appreciate, therefore, that the main priority for in-service training in the current year was the familiarisation of teachers with the new syllabuses.

The financial provision for in-service training had been very substantially increased in 1989 and would increase again in 1990 to become significantly more than double the 1988 figure. The bulk of the increased funds was being allocated to one-day in-service courses held in February, March and November in connection with the introduction of the new Junior Certificate. Over 14 000 teachers had attended the courses in various centres throughout the country. For 1990 a similar, major in-service programme was planned and, again, the bulk of the financial provision would be devoted to it. In the short term, priority in in-service training for second-level teachers would be given to ensuring familiarity with the syllabuses and methodologies of the new Junior Certificate course.

At the primary level, there was a good deal more in-service work going on than might appear from the small budget allocated for the purpose. Most in-service work consisted of one-week courses in the summer, for which teachers got three days extra personal vacation during the school year following, rather than being paid travel and subsistence allowances. In addition, since much of the planning and supervision of in-service courses was currently carried out by the Department's inspectors, costs were below the line. About 9 000 teachers attended these courses each year.

The examiners had made the point that in-service training was often assumed to refer to short and intensive courses, and argued rightly for a wider understanding so that it might embrace the concept of career-long development of teachers, an approach to teacher formation with which the Minister strongly concurred. A first consideration concerned whether INSET should remain voluntary. The examiners thought it should be a requirement, and she could see the logic of that, given that it might often be the teacher most needing further professional development who was the most reluctant to take advantage of the training courses available. She believed that such a significant change in the approach to INSET would require extensive and, she suspected, difficult discussions with the teacher unions and providers. Accordingly, she would prefer, first of all, to see how much could be achieved by developments based on voluntary participation and a more attractive range of in-service offerings.

One of the Minister's concerns in expanding the provision for INSET and, especially, in moving towards the concept of a "teaching career", was that purposeful planning by individual teachers of their participation in training should be matched by a similarly structured and farsighted framework of provision at the national level. The examiners had indicated the need for a national body and, while she certainly agreed on the necessity for a national approach, she believed that it would be a mistake to distance the planning of INSET from curricular planning generally, of which it was, surely, an integral part. Consequently, Ireland's approach was to incorporate responsibility for the overall planning and provision of INSET within the remit of the National Council for Curriculum and Assessment, as an extension of the work it was already undertaking in relation to the new Junior Certificate. In this way the development of curriculum and orientation of the teachers who would deliver it could progress in step, with due regard for the realities of the classroom.

The *delegate of the United Kingdom* said that the central funding of INSET was problematic; it could become a black hole since there was such a variety of training needs. INSET should be an integrated part of a general strategy for change. *Professor Smith* intervened to agree that INSET should not be equated with pulling out individual teachers for training. Research findings showed that excellent results came from training programmes involving all the personnel in a school.

The *delegate of Switzerland* asked about the articulation between pre-service and in-service training, and whether teachers and their unions were in favour of obligatory training. The *Minister* replied that pre-service and in-service training had so far been regarded as distinct. There had been no conception of INSET as obligatory on the part of any of the principal actors. The unions wished to have more INSET but on a voluntary basis. Attendance at a three-day training course had been de facto mandatory for some primary school teachers.

6. TRAINING FOR LEADERSHIP AND MANAGEMENT

Professor Smith said it seemed that only tentative and *ad hoc* efforts had been made so far to prepare principals and senior staff in the schools for their onerous duties. *Did the national authorities accept the view of the examiners that pre-training and continuing training were required for all those who exercised special responsibilities in schools? If so, what kind of arrangements were envisaged?*

Important personal and procedural changes were taking place in the management and governance of schools in Ireland. At the same time, parents were becoming increasingly active in school affairs. *In view of these developments what kind of briefing and training arrangements were envisaged by the national authorities?*

The examiners, replied the *Minister*, had quite correctly highlighted the importance of school management in providing effective schooling and the concomitant need for extensive training in school leadership. There was no doubt that school leadership and management were increasingly demanding tasks for which at least some principals and senior teachers were ill prepared. In addition, financing for responsibility posts was made available but such posts had not contributed in the main to a strong middle-management structure.

As she had indicated in an earlier response, it was the authorities' intention to devolve significant responsibility for day-to-day school management matters to schools, and this would imply a reassessment of the roles of senior school staff and the establishment of functional internal structures. One of the priorities for INSET provision, therefore, would be courses in leadership and management. While some such courses had been run both by her Department and under its auspices, a significant expansion of leadership and management training would be required in the near future if schools were to be able to respond to the assumption of greater autonomy, and, it must be emphasized, greater responsibility for their own affairs.

An encouraging development in the current year had been the inauguration of a Diploma in Educational Administration by one of the university departments of education. Other teacher training institutions had also shown considerable interest in training in this area.

The *delegate of France* was interested in the election of parents to school boards. Could a parent become the chairman of a board? Could parents help devise school plans? Was there a hidden hierarchy? The *Minister* replied that parents might be elected to primary school boards, but were unlikely to become chairpersons. At the secondary level parents sat on most school boards and might become chairpersons in the future. There was no "hidden hierarchy".

7. CONCLUDING REMARKS

Professor Skilbeck believed that the lively discussion before the Education Committee had revealed an education system that was actively renewing itself and an Irish delegation that was fully alert to the issues and problems raised by the examiners and members of the Committee. The central question was whether the education service as a whole was ready and able to respond to the challenges that faced it. Societal needs and expectations were very high, and a great effort would be required to implement the changes that were agreed to be desirable. New roles were being foreseen for the schools within a national framework of goals, values, curriculum and structures.

The *Minister* had agreed that it was necessary to look into the adequacy of existing resources and to order priorities. The machinery for overall policy-making would be strengthened. The National Council for Curriculum and Assessment was to have a wider remit. For the Inspectorate a developmental support and intelligence-gathering role was envisaged. The Minister did not see the necessity, however, for an intermediate administrative level between the Department of Education and the schools, but felt that the schools should assume greater administrative powers.

The Minister had pointed to ways of addressing the problem of surplus teacher training capacity. The training colleges should not be closed down, but diversified. There was complete agreement that maintaining teacher quality and effectiveness was essential for educational reform. The Minister had thus given a very positive endorsement to the proposal to strengthen in-service education and training, including the training of principals, school managers and parents to undertake their new roles. However, the balance between available resources and the wide and diverse needs of INSET remained uncertain, and much planning and development were required.

The pupil/teacher ratio would be progressively reduced while bearing in mind the priority of improving conditions in schools with particular disadvantages. On curricular reform, the Minister had referred to the inquiries that were in progress and modifications to the national examinations. The needs of underachievers would continue to require special attention.

All those present must have been encouraged by the Minister's positive approach to problems and difficulties, and openness to fresh ideas. She had spoken throughout like a true educator.

Part Three

SUMMARY OF THE BACKGROUND REPORT

Prepared for the review by the Irish authorities

Introduction

The Background Report is primarily intended to provide the examiners and other interested parties with a short, up-to-date description of the Irish education system, especially in so far as it concerns teacher education and supply. In addition, it includes information on the most recent forecasts of pupil and teacher numbers up to the year 2001.

With the exception of two commissioned chapters, the Report was prepared by the Department of Education. The views expressed in the two commissioned chapters (Chapters 8 and 9) are those of the authors and do not necessarily reflect those of the Department of Education. Chapter 8, by Dr. John Sheehan of University College, Dublin, examines the relationship between education and the economy. In Chapter 9, Professor John Coolahan, Professor of Education in St. Patrick's College, Maynooth, presents his view of current issues and problems in education in Ireland.

1. BACKGROUND AND CONTEXT

The island of Ireland is situated in the north-west of Europe between latitude 57.5 and 55.5 north and 5.5 and 10 west longitude. It has been extensively inhabited for more than 5 000 years. The most significant original inhabitants were the Celts, whose influence can still be seen in the culture, and on the spoken language of the country. The island was partitioned in 1920, with six of the thirty-two counties remaining part of the United Kingdom; the remainder of the island adopted its present constitution in 1937 and became a Republic in 1949.

The average population density in the Republic is under 50 per square kilometre, and the total population is 3.54 million. Up to the 1970s there was continuing emigration, mainly to the United Kingdom and the United States of America, but during that decade there was net immigration to the country, as more people came into the country than left, and the population increased rapidly. However, the birth rate has fallen sharply since 1980 and emigration, especially of young people, has increased substantially as a result of the general economic downturn.

Ireland is a parliamentary democracy with a written Constitution. It has two houses of Parliament *(Oireachtas)*, an elected President *(Uachtaran)* who is Head of State, though with very limited powers, and a Prime Minister *(Taoiseach)* who is Head of Government. The first official language of the country is Irish, though English, as the second official language, is, in fact, the everyday language of the vast majority of the population.

On achieving independence in 1922 Ireland was primarily an underdeveloped agricultural country with more than 50 per cent of the workforce employed in agricultural occupations. By 1986 this had fallen to 16 per cent, industrial employment had risen to 28 per cent and service employment to 56 per cent. While traditional industry was largely labour-intensive and native-owned, over the last 30 years considerable efforts have been made to establish new (highly productive and largely foreign-owned) industries, often in locations remote from traditional centres of industry. Since the 1920s unemployment has rarely fallen below 5 per cent and is currently running at about 17 per cent. Following on the second OPEC oil price rise in 1979, the Irish economy suffered a severe downturn and the public borrowing requirement increased substantially as a percentage of GNP, since current expenditure, much of it attempting to alleviate growing unemployment, was being supported by this means. Recent government policies, aimed at establishing and subsequently reducing the debt/GNP ratio, have resulted in restrictions on public expenditure and a demand for "value" for public expenditure in terms of achieving desirable employment targets.

2. THE SYSTEM OF EDUCATION IN IRELAND

The Constitution recognises the right and duty of parents to provide for their children's education and obliges the State to ensure that children receive a certain minimum education by providing for free first-level education. In practice, free education is provided up to the age of 18 years, largely through private or corporatively-owned schools for which state funding is available. There are comparatively few state-owned educational institutions, though there is a high degree of state control of provision and planning.

There are almost 1 million young people within the educational system at all levels (28 per cent of the population). Beyond the period of compulsory education (age 6 to 15), there is a reasonable balance of participation between males and females (however, in first level teacher training, females outnumber males by more than three to one). Participation in post-compulsory education has greatly increased in the last twenty years with numbers in the second level senior cycle almost quadrupling. In the same period participation in the third level has increased by almost 300 per cent.

Children may be admitted to first level schools at age 4 and begin the first compulsory class at 6, transfer to second level at age 12 and complete the compulsory period after 3 years in second level schools. Advancement to the next higher class is normally automatic, and without an end-of-year examination. The normal duration of second level is 5 years, and more than 70 per cent of pupils complete this period.

The Department of Education is responsible for almost all educational activity in the State. The management of education is heavily centralised (though most schools are privately-owned, and teacher appointments are not the direct responsibility of the Department of Education), there being local education authorities only for the vocational sector. There is no over-arching legislative act for the education system and most decisions are communicated by Department circulars, rather than by legislative act. The Inspectorate is composed of Primary (first level), Post-primary (second level) Inspectors, and the Psychological Service reports to and is part of the Department of Education.

Pre-school and first level education

Most pre-school is not part of the formal education system, though some forms of provision are supported by state funds (the first two years of first level schooling are designated as "infant" classes). Education at first level is provided almost exclusively through national schools, almost all of which are state-aided parish schools. Most of the 3 000+ schools are mixed, having more than 20 000 teachers of whom 16 000 are females. Responsibility for the day-to-day management of each school lies with Boards of Management comprising elected and appointed representations of the Patron, parents and teachers. Teachers are employed by the Boards of Management, though they are paid by the State. The current pupil/teacher ratio (PTR) is approximately 27.5:1 and the average class size in ordinary classes is 31 children. However, since the actual staffing of schools is related to, inter alia, the size of the school, actual figures may not necessarily reflect the situation in particular schools. Remedial and other specialist teachers are normally additional to quota.

The current curriculum at first level, which was introduced in 1971, reflects a child-centred approach to curriculum, allowing teachers considerable freedom of implementation within broad guidelines. In recent years a policy of coeducation has been introduced and special attention is being given to the needs of socially and educationally-disadvantaged pupils. Reviews of the primary curriculum, and of the organisation of first level education generally, are currently taking place.

Second level education

General second level education is provided in (private) secondary schools and in (public) vocational, comprehensive and community schools. While average school size has increased significantly over the last twenty years, some one-quarter of all schools have fewer than 250 pupils and more than half of vocational schools have fewer than 300 pupils. Almost all public schools are mixed and an increasing number, currently 30 per cent, of secondary schools admit both sexes. Secondary schools are private institutions conducted by boards of governors, religious authorities or communities (the majority) or by individuals. Almost all are denominational. The State pays more than 95 per cent of the teachers' salaries and, in addition to providing capitation fees for the majority of pupils, pays for almost all buildings and equipment costs.

There are 38 Vocational Education Committees (VECs) responsible for technical and some general second level schools education in their areas (26 counties and some of the larger towns and cities). VECs are appointed by the elected local authorities in their areas. Over 90 per cent of VEC funding comes from the State, the remainder largely from local funds. Each VEC appoints a Chief Executive Officer (CEO) who directs the organisation and administration of the system.

Comprehensive and community schools were first established in the mid-1960s as part of a policy of comprehensivisation of second level provision. They are owned and wholly funded by the State, though locally managed. At present the schools cater for about 13 per cent of all second level pupils.

Teacher allocation is usually described in terms of PTR, though, as at first level, the actual allocation is more complex, since it usually includes a number of posts related to size, specialisation, or exceptional circumstances. In the vocational sector, allocation is by committee area, rather than by school, as is the case in the other sectors. The current PTR in second level schools is 20:1. Actual rates are somewhat lower.

Many vocational schools provide ordinary junior and senior courses as well as specialist technical courses related to specific occupations. Traditionally, these would have been craft-based but now encompass commercial and secretarial occupations as well as the more traditional technical areas. In addition, a network of regional technical colleges was established in major population centres throughout the country in the late 1960s and these, together with the specialist VEC colleges in e.g. Dublin and Cork, provide higher technical and technological courses, in some cases to degree level.

The curricula in the different types of second level schools tend to be broadly similar, though with a greater emphasis on technical/vocational subjects in comprehensive and community schools and especially in vocational schools. All junior cycle pupils would be expected to study the two indigenous languages (Irish and English) and Mathematics, and most would also take History and Geography, a science subject and a modern language (most frequently French) and, in most cases, one or more "practical" subjects, up to eight or nine subjects in all. At senior cycle there is a greater range of subjects, though fewer are usually chosen.

Almost all second level schools offer syllabuses leading to the (state) public examinations taken at 15 and 17. At the end of junior cycle, two examinations currently exist: the Day Vocational Certificate (once the prerogative of the vocational sector, but now taken by many pupils in secondary schools, often at 14), and the Intermediate Certificate, now taken by almost all 15 year-olds. The Leaving Certificate examination, taken at the end of senior cycle, acts both as a terminal examination for second level education and a selection mechanism for entry to third level courses ("points" are awarded for grades achieved and added to establish eligibility for entry to specific courses). A new junior cycle programme, leading to a new Junior Certificate examination, and replacing existing junior cycle syllabuses was initiated in September 1989, and both the Day Vocational and the Intermediate Certificates will be replaced by the new examination in 1992.

Special provision for the physically and mentally handicapped is offered in a wide range of specialist centres throughout the country. Most physically handicapped pupils attend their local schools and significant attempts have been made in recent years to promote the integration of such pupils. The far more numerous mentally handicapped children (1.5 per cent of the school-going population) attend either special schools (approximately 70) or special classes within ordinary schools. Socially disadvantaged groups, such as Travellers, are also provided for in special classes in primary schools or, in the case of older children, in special centres. Remedial education is provided at both levels by teachers working in ordinary schools, either with small groups of pupils or on a team-teaching basis.

Pupil guidance in second level schools is provided by specially-trained (one year post-graduate) teachers working in individual schools. Larger schools are entitled to employ such teachers as an addition to their "quota" of teachers, in other schools they work within the overall staff allocation for the school. Guidance teachers (the official title) provide a wide range of services ranging from information on employment and further education and training to testing and personal counselling.

The youth unemployment rate in Ireland is currently 21 per cent, which is close to the EEC average of 18 per cent (April 1989). However, the likelihood of unemployment is closely related to educational level, young people leaving school with no qualifications being almost three times as likely to be unemployed as leavers with Leaving Certificate qualifications. Accordingly, a number of programmes targeted on school-leavers have been developed in recent years by both the education and labour agencies, culminating in the offering of a Social Guarantee (of full-time programmes of training or work experience of at least one year's duration). Priority for this provision was assigned to 15 year-old leavers, especially those with no formal education qualifications and, within the last year, the Departments of Education and Labour have instituted a joint programme of training and job placement aimed at this group, known as "Youthreach", which is of two years' duration. Within education, the principal "transition" programme is known as the Vocational Preparation and Training programme (VPT) and is offered, at one level, to 15 year-old leavers and also, at another level, to senior cycle leavers to find employment. There are currently some 19 000 young people on these one-year programmes, roughly divided evenly between the two levels.

While the Department of Education retains overall responsibility for curriculum and has, up to recently, been responsible for "rolling" reform of curriculum, much of the innovative work on curricula has been carried out by the curriculum centres in Dublin, Galway and Shannon and, latterly, in the first level teacher training college in Limerick. The three older centres have been almost exclusively concerned with curriculum at second level, and have initiated a wide range of curriculum innovations, covering between them most aspects of second level curricula. However, with the establishment of the National Council for Curriculum and Assessment, responsibility for advising on the initiation of curricular reform proposals has passed to that body.

A national Curriculum and Examination Board (CEB) was established on an interim basis in 1984 with a broad remit to "report on the desirable aims, structure and content of curriculum at first and second levels". It was originally proposed that responsibility for public examinations would pass to the Board, but, when the Board was reconstituted as the National Council for Curriculum and Assessment in 1987 with an advisory role in relation to curricula and assessment, it was decided that responsibility for public examinations would remain with the Department of Education. Most of the work of the Council to date, building on and developing the recommendations of the CEB, has been on the development of the new Junior Certificate referred to above.

Third level education

There are four universities in the Republic of Ireland. All are self-governing institutions which receive state grants for current and capital expenditure. The National University of Ireland has three constituent colleges (in Dublin, Cork and Galway) and recognises St. Patrick's College, Maynooth, an ecclesiastical college which admits lay students. The others are the University of Dublin (Trinity College), and the (newly-established) Dublin City University and the University of Limerick. Higher technological education is provided in the Dublin Institute of Technology (which comprises six colleges and is administered by the City of Dublin VEC), in nine regional technical colleges throughout the country (also administered by their area VEC) and in a small number of other VEC-run colleges. First level teacher training is offered in specialist teacher training colleges in Dublin (four) and Limerick (one). These colleges are associated with the universities and offer degree-level courses. Second level teachers are trained either on post-graduate higher diploma courses or in specialist teacher training colleges. The Higher Education Authority assists in co-ordinating state funds for higher education and reviews the demand and need for higher education.

Adult and community education

Vocational Education Committees have a major responsibility for the development and provision of adult education services in their areas. In addition, many third level colleges are actively involved in the provision of extra-mural courses and distance-learning facilities. VECs are now establishing Adult Education Boards to oversee and administer adult and community education provision.

Student support

First level and most second level schools provide education free of charge, and a school transport system, mainly for rural pupils, is provided on a subsidised basis. A scheme of aid towards the cost of school books also exists and is availed of by some 26 per cent of pupils. Means-tested student support schemes exist at third level and, in addition, grants (not means-tested) are available for participants on a range of European Social Fund-supported programmes. In 1987 almost 50 per cent of third level students received some level of grant aid.

3. THE NATURE OF SCHOOL PROVISION

There are over 3 000 first level and 800 second level schools in Ireland, widely dispersed throughout the country with many quite small towns having several first and second level schools. There are over 800 one- or two-teacher first level schools, and some 140 second level schools (mainly in the vocational sector) have under 200 pupils. Despite the extensive building programme of the last two decades, many schools at both levels have buildings more than 20 years old, though a large number would have new extensions for science or technical subjects. At second level almost all schools attempt to offer as wide a range of subjects as possible and there is little in the way of sharing resources or staff between schools, except in the vocational sector where some specialist teachers may work in several (vocational) schools in an area.

First level schools are requested to be "in operation" for a minimum of 184 days and secondary, comprehensive and community schools, 180 days (vocational schools tend to operate the same number of days). The 12 days of the public examinations may be included as part of the 180 days at second level. Most schools have mid-term breaks, of up to one week in the first and second terms. Schools operate mainly on a five-day week basis, of some 22 hours' duration at first and 30 hours at second level. Schools usually begin at 9.00 a.m. and end not later than 4.00 p.m. (earlier in the case of first level schools).

At first level, the curriculum offered includes Religion (as prescribed by the appropriate denominational authority), Irish, English, Mathematics, Social and Environmental Studies, Art and Crafts, Music and Physical Education. The syllabuses are outlined in official handbooks provided by the Department of Education. Except in a few schools, all teaching of a class is conducted by a single class teacher. At second level, while a wide range of subjects is available, most teachers are specialist subject teachers and, consequently, outside of the core subjects, the range of curricular provision would reflect the subject specialisation of the teaching staff, except, as already indicated, in the case of vocational schools. In junior (compulsory) cycle Irish, English and Mathematics are obligatory and more than 80 per cent of schools offer History/Geography, Civics, Science, Physical Education, Art and French. The next most popular language, German, is offered in 21 per cent of schools. A broadly similar range of provision is offered in senior cycle, though more subjects are available. Recent studies have shown that, at second level, boys' schools tend to be highly specialised in Science, honours Mathematics and Commerce, whereas girls' schools tend to offer a more general range of subjects. Because vocational school teachers can be shared between such schools in an area, despite the relatively small size of many vocational schools, they offer a wide range of subjects, albeit often in quite small classes.

Many teachers play an important part in the promotion of extra-curriculum activities for their pupils, especially games. At first level the team games of hurling and football are strongly supported as are a range of other games and community activities. At second level also, many teachers support school team "games" activities and also a wide range of pupils' hobbies and interest groups. Music and dance are also strongly supported in many schools.

Increasingly, parents are actively involved in Boards of Management of schools, formally so in the case of first level schools. Many schools have parent or parent/teacher associations which promote school activities and often support schools' fund-raising. At national level, a National Parents' Council, established with Department of Education support in 1985, is active at first and second levels in promoting the interests of parents and their children.

4. THE COST OF EDUCATION

The Irish education system is predominantly state funded. The contribution of private persons, through personal costs and in the form of fees (at third level), is, however, significant. Because of a shortage of suitable data, the non-state component of education spending cannot be accurately stated, and is not estimated here. It should therefore be borne in mind that education spending as a percentage of GNP is somewhat larger than shown.

Education spending rose from 2.38 per cent of GNP in 1961, to almost 7 per cent in 1987, and has since declined to an estimated 6.13 per cent in 1989. At the same time, overall public spending rose rather more slowly, from 20.41 per cent of GNP in 1961 to a peak of 41.68 per cent in 1983, declining to an estimated 32.2 per cent in 1989. Education spending rose more rapidly, and has fallen more slowly, than general public spending, because of the huge expansion of education in the 1960s and 1970s, and because some 81.5 per cent of education spending is now accounted for by pay, which is not readily susceptible to rapid reduction.

The recurrent cost per pupil in 1989 is estimated to be I£ 850 at first level, I£ 1 453 at second level, and I£ 3 248 at third level. Since 1961/62, the cost at second level has risen somewhat more than that at first level because of the introduction of free second level education in 1967.

Teacher training costs are somewhat higher than the general cost of third level education, largely because of falling numbers of entrants to teacher training in recent years. The average annual cost of specialist teacher training (excluding those who train in general university courses), is now between I£ 5 500 and I£ 6 000, with a total cost per trained teacher between I£ 18 500 and I£ 23 000.

Direct expenditure on research and development, and on "quality control" in the form of inspection of schools and teachers, accounts for about 0.8 per cent of the total education budget.

When Ireland's spending on education is expressed as a percentage of GNP, the level of expenditure compares well with other European countries, at between 6 and 7 per cent of GNP throughout the 1980s.

The future direction of education spending will be determined by the overall restriction on public spending; by declining enrolments at first and second levels; and by a clear trend towards increased demand for third level and post-second level education with a technological and vocational emphasis.

5. THE EDUCATION AND TRAINING OF TEACHERS

First level pre-service training

Up to 1987 there were six colleges of education responsible for training of teachers for first level schools. One has now closed. All are denominational in character and privately owned. They are funded by grants from the Department of Education (for current and capital expenditure) and students fees. All are associated with one or other of the universities and offer training leading to a Bachelor of Education. Recruitment is on the basis of Leaving Certificate examination results and a central interview. Successful candidates would have achieved relatively high scores in the Leaving Certificate examinations and would be eligible, had they wished, to select many of the more demanding university courses.

Courses offered are broadly similar in all colleges except that those associated with the National University of Ireland offer an honours degree after 3 years, while those associated with the University of Dublin require 4 years. Courses are a combination of theory and practice involving study of a range of subjects including Education and practical experience under the supervision of staff members. This takes place during the three years of the course, typically of 3-4 weeks per year, in first level schools surrounding the college.

Second level pre-service training

There are twelve institutions offering pre-service training for second level teachers, though, in practice, more than 80 per cent are trained in the National

University of Ireland or the University of Dublin. The other institutions are concerned with the training of teachers of specific specialist subjects. University-trained teachers generally take a basic (Bachelor) degree over 3 or 4 years and then attend a one-year full-time course leading to a Higher Diploma in Education. As might be expected, most graduates teach in the more traditional academic disciplines. Up to the early 1970s teachers of practical (vocational) subjects were trained on courses organised directly by the Department of Education. However, qualifications for teachers of these subjects and of other specialist subjects such as Art, Home Economics and Catechism are now obtained in specialist colleges, in some cases dedicated to teacher training.

In general, a pattern of open entry applies to university-based (post-graduate) teacher training courses. In the case of the other colleges, requirements vary between colleges, since they recruit second level school-leavers. Where the colleges are associated with University Colleges, the minimum requirements for entry to these colleges normally apply.

The Higher Diploma in Education courses are of one year's duration and focus on the theory and practice of education in schools. All courses require students to undertake teaching practice in second level schools (approximately 100 hours). Since the entry qualifications to secondary teaching are laid down by the Registration Council (see below), the Council's guidelines for teacher training are broadly followed by all trainers, including those not affiliated to the universities.

Induction, probation and in-service

There are no formal induction procedures for teachers in Ireland, though very many schools offer some informal support to newly-appointed staff members. Teachers are first appointed as "probationers" and there are formal procedures for admitting such teachers to full-time incremental posts following successful completion of probation, which normally lasts one year. A number of teaching bodies have drawn up recommendations to schools concerning the need for proper support and monitoring of probationary teachers.

While the nature of in-service provision is different in first and second level teaching, such provision is provided either directly or indirectly by the central authority (Department of Education). In recent years, also, the development of curriculum projects, especially at second level, has made it possible to use teacher participation in these activities as an influential form of in-service training. In addition, there is a recent tendency for in-service to be provided by a variety of interested bodies, with central support and monitoring, rather than directly by the Department's inspectorate. At first level, teacher attendance at in-service courses "earns" additional leave during school time, since courses are normally conducted during the summer holiday period. At second level there is no such leave allowance though, unlike at first level, expenses are paid and attendance is nearly always voluntary, except for the introduction of the new Junior Certificate courses. Courses range from one-day seminars to four-week intensive programmes. Overall, some 9 000 first level and more than 5 000 second level teachers attend such courses annually.

In recent years the importance of in-service education for teachers has been acknowledged by a number of sources, including the 1980 White Paper on Educational Development. A recent report on in-service highlighted the relative decline in provision in recent years (now reversed), and the low level of in-service activity in Ireland by comparison with other countries. It also called for a greater involvement of pre-service institutions in in-service provision, and called for the establishment of a national council for in-service training.

6. THE EMPLOYMENT OF TEACHERS

The chapter in the Background Report sets out in some detail the salary and conditions of employment of teachers, the nature of posts of responsibility, and how teachers' work is appraised.

Entry to teaching

At first level, most entrants are graduates of one of the recognised teacher training colleges described in Chapter 5. Selection is made by a Selection Board appointed by the Board of Management. Teachers in secondary schools are required to have passed the conditions of registration laid down by the Registration Council (a legally-established body representative of university, school management and teaching bodies and the Minister for Education, which regulates the registration of teachers to work in secondary schools). Since secondary schools are private institutions, procedures for selection are a matter for the individual school authorities. Vocational teachers are appointed by a Selection Board nominated by the VEC and are required to have a teaching subject in their degree, or, if specialists, to hold a recognised teaching diploma in their specialism. Teachers in community and comprehensive schools are also appointed by Selection Boards and have similar qualifications to those in the other sectors of second level education.

Employment of teachers

All teachers are employed by their individual school managements or, in the case of vocational teachers, by their VECs, though their salaries are, in effect, paid by the State and they are classified, for e.g. tax purposes, as civil servants. (However, secondary teachers receive a small percentage of their salaries from their school authorities.) There is a common basic scale for all teachers (a 26-year scale). In addition, teachers receive allowances for their level of qualification (though not level of teaching). At first level, teachers are required to be present during the entire school day. At second level, teachers, while normally present for the school day, are required to engage in between 18 and 23 hours of class contact per week.

There is a scheme of conciliation and arbitration in operation for all teachers' pay. The recommendations of the Arbitration Board must be presented by the Ministers for Education and Finance to the *Dail* (Parliament) with the intention of either accepting the recommendations, or accompanied by a motion to reject or modify the recommendations.

In addition to the posts of Principal and Vice-Principal, most schools have other posts of responsibility for teachers, normally filled on the basis of seniority. These posts carry allowances and the number in each school is determined by a system of points computed for each school on the basis of the (weighted) numbers of pupils. Posts of responsibility may be for a number of school functions, though not for the supervision or monitoring of the work of other teachers.

Teacher appraisal

The appraisal of probationary teachers in first level schools is conducted by members of the Department of Education inspectorate during visits to the schools to observe the teachers in their classrooms. There is a formal procedure, agreed with the teacher union, for the probation of these teachers, normally after one year. At second level a formal inspection report is not a requirement for the successful completion of probation and, in practice, because of staffing shortages, only a relatively small number of such teachers are inspected.

At first level, inspection of probated teachers is conducted on a regular basis by the Primary Inspectorate, usually for the purpose of preparing School Reports. At second level, since both teachers and inspectors are specialists, inspection of individual teachers is normally part of an evaluation of particular subject teaching in the schools.

Most inspection work at first level is concerned with the appraisal of school functioning, and the preparation of School Reports. These reports are normally the basis of discussion between the inspectors concerned and the staff and would constitute an opportunity for school review. Similar "organisation inspections" are carried out at second level, but without the same formal feedback to school staff (though a summary of the report is sent to the school authorities).

7. THE SUPPLY OF AND DEMAND FOR TEACHERS

The education system expanded rapidly in the 1960s and 1970s. This trend stopped in the 1980s, and has reversed in recent years. One consequence is that there are relatively few teachers in the 20-30 age band, and the modal age at all levels is now between 30 and 40. Another consequence is that the pattern of behaviour of newly-qualified teachers has changed, so that many of them now tend to seek employment other than teaching within a short time of graduating.

The best estimates of population trends indicate that the population of Ireland will fall between now and 2006. In addition, enrolment in full-time education is predicted to fall at all levels. First level has already started its decline; second level is projected to remain more or less static up to 1994/95 and then decline; and only at third level is there a prospect of increasing enrolments up to the late 1990s.

In parallel to the reduction in enrolments, the number of teachers required at first and second levels will decline. By 2000/01, the number of first level teachers needed may be 20 per cent less than in 1987/88. At second level the decline will be less, perhaps 10 per cent.

The projected rate of decline in enrolments matches fairly well the likely decline in the number of teachers through natural wastage (age, retirement, death, change of job, etc.). As a consequence, the demand for newly-trained teachers is likely to be very small for the next ten years. In 1987, of the teachers graduating from specialist training colleges, only 11.4 per cent found permanent wholetime teaching posts. Graduates trained in the Universities fared even worse, with 5.4 per cent finding permanent wholetime teaching employment. Medium-term prospects show no sign of an improvement.

At first level, the outlook is particularly poor in the short and medium term because the decline in enrolments has already manifested itself. The probability is that new graduates will enter teaching, if at all, by spending increasing lengths of time as substitutes, perhaps to the point where some will never obtain permanent employment. At second level the outlook is a little better up to about 1995. Some new graduates will continue to be needed up to that point, although in considerably smaller numbers than heretofore. After the mid-1990s, there is likely to be little or no demand up to the turn of the century.

It is significant that relatively large numbers of newly qualified teachers do not enter teaching at all at present, and the speed with which they find other employment indicates that they may not seriously seek teaching employment. In addition, the completion of the internal market in 1992 should open up new prospects of employment in the EEC generally. Finally, the present structure of the age profile of teachers will result in rapid ageing, so that by the year 2000, the average teacher will have spent some 25 years teaching since completing training. For these reasons, a simple relationship between a decline in demand for teachers and in demand for teacher training facilities cannot be presumed.

8. EDUCATION AND THE ECONOMY

This chapter was prepared by John Sheehan, Department of Political Economy, University College, Dublin. The chapter represents his views.

Attitudes of economic policy-makers to education

The author argues that, prior to the original Investment in Education report, prepared for the OECD in 1965, the view was that the principal objective of education was seen as the cultural and moral development of the child "rather than the practical", to quote from one publication of the time. Following on that report and, especially, in the 1980s, a series of government publications emphasized the manpower and vocational aspects of education and the need for development to be influenced by manpower criteria. The current National Development Plan (1989-1993) places considerable emphasis on training, especially in the areas of language, managerial and technical skills. Significantly, in his view, it makes little distinction, in this area, between education and training in the traditional sense of the terms.

Economic analysis and educational policy

In this section, the author discusses the international literature on the economics of education. He discusses the Human Capital model which he claims has influenced policy-making on education in Ireland over the last twenty years, and he analyses a wide range of publications, mainly from the United Kingdom and the United States of America, concerning personal and social rates of return to education. He argues that there is a consensus in the literature concerning the benefits to the individual of increased investment in education. He quotes from one Irish study carried out in the mid-1970s which suggested that secondary education gave a higher rate of return than vocational education, that males gained more than females and that special skill training was of more benefit than an extension of traditional schooling. He also points to the concern expressed in some quarters in Ireland that competition between providers of education and training could lead to over-provision, especially in view of the availability of EEC (European Social Fund, ESF) support for certain types of training initiatives.

Some implication of EEC policies

The author draws attention to the greatly increased role of the ESF in supporting training programmes for young people in recent years. He argues that ESF funding could lead to an over-provision of places and programmes in areas attracting such aid and that distortions of provision could result. He discusses the implications of emigration within the Community of qualified young people, especially from peripheral regions (such as Ireland), to the richer areas and poses the question of the appropriateness of such transfers of resources. He suggests that there are two views on the desirability of equalising levels of education and training provision throughout the Community, one which stresses the importance of catching up and the other which cautions against overheating education and training provision in advance of countries' general economic development, and draws the implication that "unco-ordinated educational target-setting by [EEC] member states does not seem to be an optimal policy".

Determinants of educational expenditure

Public expenditure on education in 1988 was some 14.3 per cent of all Exchequer spending and 6.8 per cent of GNP. The author argues that private expenditure on education has declined over the last twenty years, from some 25 per cent to 10 per cent of total expenditure and he offers an analysis of the reasons for real growth in expenditure on education in Ireland over the last 25 years. He identifies population growth, increases in real income and the price (to pupils and parents) as the key influences. In relation to the costs of education, he argues that since education is highly labour-intensive, input costs may be an important source of increased expenditure. One of the major aspects of these costs he identifies as the continuing fall in pupil/teacher ratios over the last 25 years.

Efficiency and productivity

The author suggests that education exhibits many of the symptoms of Baumol's disease, since it is highly labour-intensive, with little scope for productivity improvement, it is a non-market provider and, hence, incentives to efficiency are minimised and the demand for quality of teaching prevents the substitution of cheaper alternatives. He summarises a number of international studies of the productivity of school systems and suggests that they show that "increased expenditures and lower pupil/teacher ratios were by themselves ineffective in educational terms". He argues that the lack of suitable data on trends in Ireland makes analysis difficult but suggests that the international experience would caution against increasing expenditure per pupil per se as a means of improving attainment.

Conclusion

In the author's view, an adequate level of general education is essential as a foundation for subsequent training and employement. He calls for a co-ordinated policy on EEC-supported programmes and for a maintenance of educational standards especially where falling rolls could lead to apparent decline in productivity.

9. A VIEW OF THE IRISH EDUCATION SYSTEM: CURRENT ISSUES AND PROBLEMS

Professor John Coolahan, Professor of Education, St. Patrick's College, Maynooth, was invited to contribute this chapter as a personal reflection on issues in education. The chapter represents his views. The summary that follows was prepared by the Department of Education and lists the main points of his essay.

At the outset Professor Coolahan emphasizes the importance of considering education in the contempory social context in Ireland and the dangers of viewing educational problems in isolation. He draws attention to the relative recency of most educational innovation in Ireland. He points to the effects of the more buoyant economy of the 1960s and early 1970s as leading to a considerable expansion in educational provision and the initiation at first level of a new child-centred curriculum and the development of closer links with the community through the establishment of Boards of Management of schools. At second level he describes the introduction of "free education", school transport and the establishment of comprehensive and, later, community schools. He also points to the difference between the recent experience in Ireland of rising numbers in education, with the opposite experience elsewhere and, as roll numbers begin to fall, of the value of studies such as this one for the planning of Irish educational policy in the 1990s.

The author identifies a number of contextual issues influencing the current educational debate:

-- *The financial situation:* current constraints on expenditure and the reduction of some educational services and a failure to make hoped-for reforms.

-- *The socio-political climate:* a shift in public attitudes to education from unreally high expectations to an "instrumentalist, utilitarian and functionalist" approach.

-- *The school in question:* a considerable expansion of participation in education at second level has not led to a concomitant improvement in the youth employment situation and up to 15 per cent of young people leave the system without any formal qualification.

-- *The socio-economic environment and the school:* recession, redundancy, unemployment and emigration have had a severe impact both on the expectations of school-leavers and on the climate of schooling itself.

-- *Population decline:* leading to uncertainty in teacher employment and school viability.

-- *Decline of the numbers of religious in education.*

-- *Increased involvement of parents:* particularly at a political level, parents, traditionally marginalised in the education debate, are beginning to play a more active role.

Current issues in the Irish education system

The Department of Education and Educational Policy in Ireland. The author contrasts the largely passive role of education ministers in the past with the current high profile of education. He points to the centralisation of policy-making and administration of education and the absence of a body of legislation or consultative agencies within the education sector and the failure to implement a series of proposals, and reports on aspects of educational provision. The importance of the Inspectorate within the system is highlighted as is the need for proper channels of communication between all the parties in education.

The Changing Role of the School. "This is the first generation in Irish history where the vast majority are experiencing such an extended encounter with schooling". A multiplicity of roles is expected of schools, while disenchantment with their ability to deliver is growing.

The planning of school provision and resources. Especially at second level, the existence of different management structures and the multiplicity of small schools can lead to considerable competition for resources and great variation in provision between different schools, even in the same area. In particular, there is a need for more positive discrimination in favour of schools in disadvantaged areas.

The continuing challenge of curricular, pedagogic and assessment reform. The author identifies a continuing need for reform of all aspects of curriculum but identifies lack of adequate funding and support as a major cause of failure to achieve widespread change. He highlights the significance of the Curriculum and Examinations Board and, later, the National Council for Curriculum and Assessment in leading the moves towards change but wonders if sufficient attention has been paid to the implementation process.

The school as a community. In recent years teaching has changed from being an isolated activity within individual classrooms to being, in many schools, a collectively-planned and -structured approach to meeting the needs of pupils and the goals of the school.

The school within the community. The importance of home-school and school-community links are stressed, especially in providing for the needs of disadvantaged young people.

Inequality in education. Despite the public commitment to equality of educational opportunity, the author claims that this has been interpreted in a very superficial way and that "socio-economic status...still influences significantly individuals' opportunities to derive benefit from the educational system".

The education of minorities. In addition to provision for the physically and mentally handicapped, the author identifies the importance of education for Travellers, and of the provision of interdenominational and all-Irish language schools.

The teachers and the challenges they face

The author believes that the inevitable reforms of the education system which will come about as a result of e.g. demographic change will make even greater demands on teachers in the future. He praises the calibre of the present teaching force and warns against a reduction in quality resulting from a lack of opportunities in teaching. Teacher education needs to be improved both by taking advantage of the reduced number of entrants to allow more intensive initial training and by greatly expanding the scope of in-service education by improved "co-operative planning between teacher education agencies, the existing teaching force and the inspectorate".

Planning for the future

The author points to the importance of having a coherent and well thought out strategy for change, especially in relation to the implementation of plans and initiatives throughout the system. He also calls for an integrated political, social and economic approach to educational planning and asserts that in the absence of a political will for reform, there is a danger of "slippage" on the gains of the past.

WHERE TO OBTAIN OECD PUBLICATIONS – OÙ OBTENIR LES PUBLICATIONS DE L'OCDE

Argentina – Argentine
CARLOS HIRSCH S.R.L.
Galería Güemes, Florida 165, 4° Piso
1333 Buenos Aires Tel. 30.7122, 331.1787 y 331.2391
Telegram: Hirsch-Baires
Telex: 21112 UAPE-AR. Ref. s/2901
Telefax:(1)331-1787

Australia – Australie
D.A. Book (Aust.) Pty. Ltd.
648 Whitehorse Road, P.O.B 163
Mitcham, Victoria 3132 Tel. (03)873.4411
Telefax: (03)873.5679

Austria – Autriche
OECD Publications and Information Centre
Schedestrasse 7
D-W 5300 Bonn 1 (Germany) Tel. (49.228)21.60.45
Telefax: (49.228)26.11.04
Gerold & Co.
Graben 31
Wien I Tel. (0222)533.50.14

Belgium – Belgique
Jean De Lannoy
Avenue du Roi 202
B-1060 Bruxelles Tel. (02)538.51.69/538.08.41
Telex: 63220 Telefax: (02) 538.08.41

Canada
Renouf Publishing Company Ltd.
1294 Algoma Road
Ottawa, ON K1B 3W8 Tel. (613)741.4333
Telex: 053-4783 Telefax: (613)741.5439
Stores:
61 Sparks Street
Ottawa, ON K1P 5R1 Tel. (613)238.8985
211 Yonge Street
Toronto, ON M5B 1M4 Tel. (416)363.3171
Federal Publications
165 University Avenue
Toronto, ON M5H 3B8 Tel. (416)581.1552
Telefax: (416)581.1743
Les Publications Fédérales
1185 rue de l'Université
Montréal, PQ H3B 3A7 Tel.(514)954-1633
Les Éditions La Liberté Inc.
3020 Chemin Sainte-Foy
Sainte-Foy, PQ G1X 3V6 Tel. (418)658.3763
Telefax: (418)658.3763

Denmark – Danemark
Munksgaard Export and Subscription Service
35, Nørre Søgade, P.O. Box 2148
DK-1016 København K Tel. (45 33)12.85.70
Telex: 19431 MUNKS DK Telefax: (45 33)12.93.87

Finland – Finlande
Akateeminen Kirjakauppa
Keskuskatu 1, P.O. Box 128
00100 Helsinki Tel. (358 0)12141
Telex: 125080 Telefax: (358 0)121.4441

France
OECD/OCDE
Mail Orders/Commandes par correspondance:
2, rue André-Pascal
75775 Paris Cédex 16 Tel. (33-1)45.24.82.00
Bookshop/Librairie:
33, rue Octave-Feuillet
75016 Paris Tel. (33-1)45.24.81.67
  (33-1)45.24.81.81
Telex: 620 160 OCDE
Telefax: (33-1)45.24.85.00 (33-1)45.24.81.76
Librairie de l'Université
12a, rue Nazareth
13100 Aix-en-Provence Tel. 42.26.18.08
Telefax : 42.26.63.26

Germany – Allemagne
OECD Publications and Information Centre
Schedestrasse 7
D-W 5300 Bonn 1 Tel. (0228)21.60.45
Telefax: (0228)26.11.04

Greece – Grèce
Librairie Kauffmann
28 rue du Stade
105 64 Athens Tel. 322.21.60
Telex: 218187 LIKA Gr

Hong Kong
Swindon Book Co. Ltd.
13 - 15 Lock Road
Kowloon, Hong Kong Tel. 366.80.31
Telex: 50 441 SWIN HX Telefax: 739.49.75

Iceland – Islande
Mál Mog Menning
Laugavegi 18, Pósthólf 392
121 Reykjavik Tel. 15199/24240

India – Inde
Oxford Book and Stationery Co.
Scindia House
New Delhi 110001 Tel. 331.5896/5308
Telex: 31 61990 AM IN
Telefax: (11)332.5993
17 Park Street
Calcutta 700016 Tel. 240832

Indonesia – Indonésie
Pdii-Lipi
P.O. Box 269/JKSMG/88
Jakarta 12790 Tel. 583467
Telex: 62 875

Ireland – Irlande
TDC Publishers – Library Suppliers
12 North Frederick Street
Dublin 1 Tel. 744835/749677
Telex: 33530 TDCP EI Telefax: 748416

Italy – Italie
Libreria Commissionaria Sansoni
Via Benedetto Fortini, 120/10
Casella Post. 552
50125 Firenze Tel. (055)64.54.15
Telex: 570466 Telefax: (055)64.12.57
Via Bartolini 29
20155 Milano Tel. 36.50.83
La diffusione delle pubblicazioni OCSE viene assicurata dalle principali librerie ed anche da:
Editrice e Libreria Herder
Piazza Montecitorio 120
00186 Roma Tel. 679.46.28
Telex: NATEL I 621427
Libreria Hoepli
Via Hoepli 5
20121 Milano Tel. 86.54.46
Telex: 31.33.95 Telefax: (02)805.28.86
Libreria Scientifica
Dott. Lucio de Biasio 'Aeiou'
Via Meravigli 16
20123 Milano Tel. 805.68.98
Telefax: 800175

Japan – Japon
OECD Publications and Information Centre
Landic Akasaka Building
2-3-4 Akasaka, Minato-ku
Tokyo 107 Tel. (81.3)3586.2016
Telefax: (81.3)3584.7929

Korea – Corée
Kyobo Book Centre Co. Ltd.
P.O. Box 1658, Kwang Hwa Moon
Seoul Tel. (REP)730.78.91
Telefax: 735.0030

Malaysia/Singapore – Malaisie/Singapour
Co-operative Bookshop Ltd.
University of Malaya
P.O. Box 1127, Jalan Pantai Baru
59700 Kuala Lumpur
Malaysia Tel. 756.5000/756.5425
Telefax: 757.3661
Information Publications Pte. Ltd.
Pei-Fu Industrial Building
24 New Industrial Road No. 02-06
Singapore 1953 Tel. 283.1786/283.1798
Telefax: 284.8875

Netherlands – Pays-Bas
SDU Uitgeverij
Christoffel Plantijnstraat 2
Postbus 20014
2500 EA's-Gravenhage Tel. (070 3)78.99.11
Voor bestellingen: Tel. (070 3)78.98.80
Telex: 32486 stdru Telefax: (070 3)47.63.51

New Zealand – Nouvelle-Zélande
GP Publications Ltd.
Customer Services
33 The Esplanade - P.O. Box 38-900
Petone, Wellington
Tel. (04)685-555 Telefax: (04)685-333

Norway – Norvège
Narvesen Info Center - NIC
Bertrand Narvesens vei 2
P.O. Box 6125 Etterstad
0602 Oslo 6 Tel. (02)57.33.00
Telex: 79668 NIC N Telefax: (02)68.19.01

Pakistan
Mirza Book Agency
65 Shahrah Quaid-E-Azam
Lahore 3 Tel. 66839
Telex: 44886 UBL PK. Attn: MIRZA BK

Portugal
Livraria Portugal
Rua do Carmo 70-74
Apart. 2681
1117 Lisboa Codex Tel.: 347.49.82/3/4/5
Telefax: (01) 347.02.64

Singapore/Malaysia – Singapour/Malaisie
See Malaysia/Singapore" – Voir «Malaisie/Singapour»

Spain – Espagne
Mundi-Prensa Libros S.A.
Castelló 37, Apartado 1223
Madrid 28001 Tel. (91) 431.33.99
Telex: 49370 MPLI Telefax: 575.39.98
Libreria Internacional AEDOS
Consejo de Ciento 391
08009-Barcelona Tel. (93) 301.86.15
Telefax: (93) 317.01.41

Sri Lanka
Centre for Policy Research
c/o Mercantile Credit Ltd.
55, Janadhipathi Mawatha
Colombo 1 Tel. 438471-9, 440346
Telex: 21138 VAVALEX CE Telefax: 94.1.448900

Sweden – Suède
Fritzes Fackboksföretaget
Box 16356
Regeringsgatan 12
103 27 Stockholm Tel. (08)23.89.00
Telex: 12387 Telefax: (08)20.50.21
Subscription Agency/Abonnements:
Wennergren-Williams AB
Nordenflychtsvägen 74
Box 30004
104 25 Stockholm Tel. (08)13.67.00
Telex: 19937 Telefax: (08)618.62.32

Switzerland – Suisse
OECD Publications and Information Centre
Schedestrasse 7
D-W 5300 Bonn 1 (Germany) Tel. (49.228)21.60.45
Telefax: (49.228)26.11.04
Librairie Payot
6 rue Grenus
1211 Genève 11 Tel. (022)731.89.50
Telex: 28356
Subscription Agency – Service des Abonnements
Naville S.A.
7, rue Lévrier
1201 Genève Tél.: (022) 732.24.00
Telefax: (022) 738.48.03
Maditec S.A.
Chemin des Palettes 4
1020 Renens/Lausanne Tel. (021)635.08.65
Telefax: (021)635.07.80
United Nations Bookshop/Librairie des Nations-Unies
Palais des Nations
1211 Genève 10 Tel. (022)734.60.11 (ext. 48.72)
Telex: 289696 (Attn: Sales) Telefax: (022)733.98.79

Taiwan – Formose
Good Faith Worldwide Int'l. Co. Ltd.
9th Floor, No. 118, Sec. 2
Chung Hsiao E. Road
Taipei Tel. 391.7396/391.7397
Telefax: (02) 394.9176

Thailand – Thaïlande
Suksit Siam Co. Ltd.
1715 Pama IV Road, Samyan
Bangkok 5 Tel. 251.1630

Turkey – Turquie
Kültur Yayinlari Is-Türk Ltd. Sti.
Atatürk Bulvari No. 191/Kat. 21
Kavaklidere/Ankara Tel. 25.07.60
Dolmabahce Cad. No. 29
Besiktas/Istanbul Tel. 160.71.88
Telex: 43482B

United Kingdom – Royaume-Uni
HMSO
Gen. enquiries Tel. (071) 873 0011
Postal orders only:
P.O. Box 276, London SW8 5DT
Personal Callers HMSO Bookshop
49 High Holborn, London WC1V 6HB
Telex: 297138 Telefax: 071 873 2000
Branches at: Belfast, Birmingham, Bristol, Edinburgh, Manchester

United States – États-Unis
OECD Publications and Information Centre
2001 L Street N.W., Suite 700
Washington, D.C. 20036-4910 Tel. (202)785.6323
Telefax: (202)785.0350

Venezuela
Libreria del Este
Avda F. Miranda 52, Aptdo. 60337
Edificio Galipán
Caracas 106 Tel. 951.1705/951.2307/951.1297
Telegram: Libreste Caracas

Yugoslavia – Yougoslavie
Jugoslovenska Knjiga
Knez Mihajlova 2, P.O. Box 36
Beograd Tel.: (011)621.992
Telex: 12466 jk bgd Telefax: (011)625.970

Orders and inquiries from countries where Distributors have not yet been appointed should be sent to: OECD Publications Service, 2 rue André-Pascal, 75775 Paris Cedex 16, France.

Les commandes provenant de pays où l'OCDE n'a pas encore désigné de distributeur devraient être adressées à : OCDE, Service des Publications, 2, rue André-Pascal, 75775 Paris Cédex 16, France.

75669-4/91

Ministry of Education & Training
MET Library
13th Floor, Mowat Block, Queen's Park
Toronto   M7A 1L2

OECD PUBLICATIONS, 2 rue André-Pascal, 75775 PARIS CEDEX 16
PRINTED IN FRANCE
(91 91 01 1) ISBN 92-64-13488-3 - No. 45491 1991